Y0-BZG-321

Understanding the intentions and tactics of an enemy is the first defense against him. In that spirit we offer this volume.

The Publishers

ISLAMIC GOVERNMENT

by
Ayatollah Ruhollah Khomeini

Translated by
Joint Publications Research Service,
Arlington, Virginia

Published by
Manor Books, Inc.
432 Park Avenue South
New York, New York 10016
No copyright is claimed on material from
United States Government publications.
Introduction copyright © 1979 by Scrambling Press
Analysis copyright © 1979 by Manor Books, Inc.

ISBN: 0-532-23166-X

Printed in the United States of America
First Manor printing—December 1979

CONTENTS

INTRODUCTION   1
FOREWORD   5
PROOF OF NEED FOR FORMING
  GOVERNMENT   17
Need for Executive Agencies   17
Methods of Great Prophet   18
Need for Continued Implementation of Laws   19
In Time of Amir of Faithful   20
Truth of Islamic Laws   20
1. Financial Laws   21
2. Defense Laws   23
3. Laws on Strictures, Blood Money, and Penalties   24
NEED FOR POLITICAL REVOLUTION   25
Need for Islamic Unity   26
Need for Rescuing Wronged and Deprived   27
Need for Formation of Government in Hadith   28
ISLAMIC SYSTEM OF GOVERNMENT   31
Distinction from Other Political Systems   31
Qualifications of Ruler   34
1. Knowledge of Islamic Law   34
2. Justice   34
Ruler in Time of Absence   36
Rule of Jurisprudent   37
Subjective Rule   38
Nascent Rule   40
Government Is Means for Achieving
  Sublime Goals   41
Qualities of Ruler Who Achieves These Goals   42
RULE OF JURISPRUDENT INDICATED
  BY HADITH   43
Successors of Prophet . . . Are Just Jurisprudents   43

A Look at Text of This Hadith   49
On Meaning of Hadith   49
JURISPRUDENTS ARE REPRESENTATIVES
    OF PROPHETS   52
Aims of Messages   53
Jurisprudents are Representatives of Messengers
    in Leading Army, Managing Society, Defending
    Nation, and Settling Disputes Among Peoples   55
Law-abiding Government   55
Who Should Be Trusted with Judiciary Tasks   58
Judiciary Matters Are Concerns of Just
    Jurisprudents   59
Who Is Authority on Events of Life   61
Phrases from Venerable Koran   64
'Umar ibn Hanzalah's (Concurrence)   68
Ban on Seeking Arbitration of Unjust Rulers   69
Moslem Ulema Are Authorities on All Matters   70
Ulema Appointed to Rule   70
Were Ulema Dismissed From Position of Rule?   72
Position of Ulema Is Always Preserved   73
Qaddah's Version [of Narration]   74
Abu al-Bakhtari's Version   75
Other Proofs   80
Proofs From al-Ridawi Jurisprudence   81
Another Proof   81
Tuhaf al-'Uqul Narrations   82
Path of Struggle for Forming Islamic Government   93
Meetings for Spreading the Principles   98
New 'Ashura'   99
Long-range Resistance   101
Reform of Religious Authorities   104
Eliminating Traces of Intellectual and
    Moral Colonialist Aggression   104
Reforming Those Who Claim Holiness   109
Purging Religious Centers   111
Expel Jurisprudents of Sultans   112
Destroying Unjust Governments   114
GLOSSARY   119
ANALYSIS   121

INTRODUCTION

On February 1, 1979, after almost fifteen years of exile, the Ayatollah Ruhollah Khomeini returned in triumph to the city of Tehran. Two weeks earlier, prompted by continuous riots, protests, and rumblings of revolution, Shah Mohammed Riza Pahlavi had fled for refuge in Egypt—in a flight that would eventually take him to Morocco, the Bahamas, Mexico, and the United States. Greeted by millions of supporters, Khomeini proclaimed the provisional Islamic government, set up the Revolutionary Council, and called upon the people of Iran to destroy the last vestiges of "the terrible monarchy and its illegal government." The world's leaders —most caught off guard by the sudden events—watched and waited to see what the Ayatollah would do next.

It didn't take long to find out. Within weeks the Ayatollah had authorized Revolutionary courts to round up and try former soldiers, police, and supporters of the Shah. After summary trials, held mostly at night under conditions of secrecy, the accused were summarily executed. In the first few months of Khomeini's rule more than six hundred former high-ranking officials from the Shah's regime were shot. Opposition newspapers were shut down, and the Ayatollah publicly condemned both capitalism and communism as "the creeds of Satanism."

But reprisals against the former regime comprised only part of the Ayatollah's plan for a new Iran. Advocating strict observance of Islamic laws, the Ayatollah urged that homosexuals, prostitutes, adulterers, and petty criminals be publicly tried, flogged, and—in some cases—executed. All women, he declared, should wear the *chador*, the full-length, traditional veil. Drugs, alcoholic drinks, tobacco, and Western music were strictly prohibited. The Ayatollah clearly

1

advocated the return to Moslem principles, to a set of laws more than thirteen hundred years old. He insisted upon total and uncompromising rejection of Western values. In Khomeini's terms the world was to be divided in the "struggle between Islam and the infidels."

In this atmosphere occurred the takeover of the American embassy in Tehran on November 4, with the seizing of sixty-three American hostages. Ostensibly the takeover was by students outraged that the former Shah had been permitted to enter the United States for cancer treatments. Students demanded the return of the Shah in exchange for the American hostages and, as soon became apparent, they acted with the full support of Khomeini. Khomeini quickly seized an opportunity to hold the United States and the Western world at bay, and he spoke loudly and boldly—some would say fanatically—for his cause. His goals were straightforward. As he had told the Italian journalist Oriana Fallaci some months earlier: "Islam means everything, also those things that, in your world, are called freedom, democracy. Yes, Islam contains everything. Islam includes everything. Islam is everything."

Who is this man? What is his program for Iran? How was he capable of engendering such powerful feeling and fanatical support among a nation of thirty-six million people? In a country with public education, a rising middle class, improved housing, and expanding industry, how was a bearded man in flowing robes able to turn back the calendar through centuries, advocating and gaining support for a fourteenth-century religion?

Some answers are obvious. Since A.D. 800 Iran has been predominantly a Moslem nation and ninety percent of the population belongs to the Shiite sect. Despite the years of dictatorial rule under a modern-minded shah who helped to establish close ties with the Western world, the people of Iran have clung to their nationalism with a fervent belief in a new nation of Islam. Equally fervent was their hatred of the

2

Shah. During his reign, while carrying out a surface modernization of Iran, the Shah amassed billions in personal fortune, subverted political activity, and condoned a vicious and hated secret police network, SAVAK, that was responsible for torture, assassination, and political intimidation. The people's resentment of the Shah's police tactics, personal fortune, and corrupt government practices led to a deepening resentment that exploded in open demonstrations in 1978. From a tiny village outside Paris, using a telephone network that linked him to mosques and religious leaders in Iran, the Ayatollah gave the commands that led to resistance and open rebellion. Followers embraced his promise of "a new nation of Islam." In driving out the Shah and welcoming home the seventy-eight-year-old Imam, Iranians were, in effect, uprooting a whole set of inimical Western influences and taking to heart a preordained set of fundamentalist Moslem teachings. Whether these teachings, and the man who expounds them, are sufficient for the running of a modern government remains to be seen.

It is certain that the Ayatollah Ruhollah Khomeini has never given up the Moslem ways. He has declared and shown his willingness to be a martyr in "the struggle between Islam and the infidels." Yet there are numerous contradictions in his character, as there must be in anyone who strives to support an age-old way of life in a modern world. Against all odds he has attempted to make a religion into a political system while making world politics out of a religion. He lives simply, eats sparingly, and follows the teachings of the Koran; yet he has conducted a revolution by long-distance telephone. He sits on a mat in the ancient holy city of Qum, yet he speaks into microphones and faces the cameras of an international press corps. A spokesman for an ancient way of life, he uses all the broadcast tools of the present age to make himself heard. Yet, in many ways, the man and his motives remain a mystery.

Here, for the first time, is the Ayatollah's plan of government for the state of Iran. Published less than two weeks

3

before he came into power, it illuminates more clearly than any news report those events that have taken place since those crisis-filled days of the revolution. In providing a perspective on today's events, it is a fascinating document, revealing a mind that is at once fanatical and coldly scheming, wise and naive, intelligent and terrifyingly biased. Here is the political future of Iran as seen by a man who, to many readers, must seem utterly incomprehensible. Yet, by bringing the world to the edge of crisis, this leader demands our attention. This is his plan. Here is his vision for the future of Iran. His words may confuse, frighten, or appall, but they cannot be ignored. An ancient religion, a modern revolution, and an inscrutable leader have been brought together by an accident of history, and part of the destiny of Iran is written in these pages.

Lessons on Jurisprudence (*al-fiqh*) in Islam Delivered by
His Eminence Imam Khomeini, Highest Shiite Religious
Authority, to Students of Theology in the Venerable al-
Najaf Under the Title of "Governance of Jurisprudent."

13 Dhi al-Qi'dah-1 Dhi al-Hijjah 1389 (1969-1970)

In the name of God, the merciful and the compassionate,
whose help we seek. God, lord of the universe, be thanked
and God's prayers be upon Muhammad, the best of mankind, and upon all his kinsmen.

FOREWORD

The Governance of Jurisprudent is a clear scientific idea that
may require no proof in the sense that whoever knows the
laws and beliefs can see its axiomatic nature. But the condition of the Moslem society, and the condition of our religious academies in particular, has driven this issue away
from the minds and it now needs to be proven again.

Since its inception, the Islamic movement was afflicted with
the Jews when they started their counter-activity by distorting the reputation of Islam, by assaulting it and by slandering it. This has continued to our present day. Then came the
role of groups that can be considered more evil than the devil
and his troops. This role emerged in the colonialist activity
which dates back to more than three centuries ago. The
colonists found in the Moslem world their long-sought
object. To achieve their colonialist ambitions, the colonists

5

sought to create the right conditions leading to the annihilation of Islam. They did not seek to turn the Moslems into Christians after driving them away from Islam because they do not believe in either. They wanted control and domination because they were constantly aware during the Crusades wars that the biggest obstacle preventing them from attaining their goals and putting their political plans on the brink of an abyss was Islam with its laws and beliefs and with the influence it exerted on people through their faith. This is why they treated Islam unjustly and harbored ill intentions toward it. The hands of the missionaries, the orientalists and of the information media—all of whom are in the service of the colonialist countries—have cooperated to distort the facts of Islam in a manner that has caused many people, especially the educated among them, to steer away from Islam and to be unable to find a way to reach Islam.

Islam is the religion of the strugglers who want right and justice, the religion of those demanding freedom and independence and those who do not want to allow the infidels to dominate the believers.

But the enemies have portrayed Islam in a different light. They have drawn from the minds of the ordinary people a distorted picture of Islam and implanted this picture even in the religious academies. The enemies' aim behind this was to extinguish the flame of Islam and to cause its vital revolutionary character to be lost, so that the Moslems would not think of seeking to liberate themselves and to implement all the rules of their religion through the creation of a government that guarantees their happiness under the canopy of an honorable human life.

They have said that Islam has no relationship whatsoever with organizing life and society or with creating a government of any kind and that it only concerns itself with the rules of menstruation and childbirth. It may contain some ethics. But beyond this, it has no bearing on issues of life and of organizing society. It is regrettable that all this has had its

6

bad effect not only on the ordinary people but also among college people and the students of theology. They misunderstand Islam and are ignorant of it. Islam has become as strange to them as alien people. It has become difficult for the missionary to familiarize people with Islam. On the other hand, there stands a line of the agents of colonialism to drown Islam with clamor and noise.

So that we may distinguish the reality of Islam from what people have come to know about it, I would like to draw your attention to the disparity between the Koran and the Hadith books on the one hand and the (theological) theses on the other hand. The Koran and the Hadith books, which are the most important sources of legislation, are clearly superior to the theses written by religious interpreters and legists because the Koran and the Hadith books are comprehensive and cover all aspects of life. The Koran phrases concerned with society's affairs are many times the phrases concerned with private worship. In any of the detailed Hadith books, you can hardly find more than three or four chapters concerned with regulating man's private worship and man's relationship with God and few chapters dealing with ethics. The rest is strongly connected with social and economic affairs, with human rights, with administration and with the policy of societies.

You, the youths who are the soldiers of Islam, must examine more thoroughly the brief statements I am making to you and must familiarize people throughout your life with the laws and rules of Islam, and must do so with every possible means: in writing, in speeches and in actions. Teach the people about the catastrophes, tragedies and enemies that have engulfed Islam since its inception. Do not hide what you know from the people and do not let people imagine that Islam is like present-day Christianity, that there is no difference between the mosque and the church and that Islam can do no more than regulate man's relationship with his God.

7

At a time when darkness prevailed over the Western countries, when American Indians were inhabiting America, when absolute regimes exercising domination and racial discrimination and resorting to the excessive use of force with total disregard for the public opinion and for the laws were in existence in the Roman and Persian empires—at that time, God made laws which he revealed to the greatest prophet, Muhammad, may God's peace and prayers be upon him, so that man may be born under their canopy. Everything has its ethics and its laws. Before man's birth and until the time he is lowered into his grave, laws have been drawn up to govern him. Social relationships have been drawn up and government has been organized, in addition to determining the duties of worship. Rights in Islam are high-level, complete and comprehensive rights. Jurists have often quoted the Islamic rules, laws and regulations on dealings, permissibles, punishment, jurisdiction; on regulating relations between states and peoples, on war and peace and on human rights.

Islam has thus dealt with every aspect of life and has given its judgment on it. But the foreigners have whispered to the hearts of people, especially the educated among them: "Islam possesses nothing. Islam is nothing but a bunch of rules on menstruation and childbirth. Theology students never go beyond these issues in their specialization." It is true that some students pay greater attention to this, and they are wrong in doing so. This (excessive attention) at times helps the enemies to achieve their goals. This makes the enemies, who have been working for hundreds of years to plant the seeds of negligence in our scientific academies so as to attain their goals against us and their goals in our wealth and in the resources of our country, rejoice.

At times, the foreigners whisper to the people: "Islam is deficient. Its judiciary laws are not what they should be." To further deceive and mislead the people, the agents of the British tried, on the instructions of their masters, to import foreign positional laws in the wake of the well-known revo-

8

lution and of the establishment of a constitutional regime in Iran. When they wanted to draw up the country's basic law—meaning the constitution—those agents resorted to Belgian laws which they borrowed from the Belgian Embassy. A number of those agents, whom I do not wish to name, copied those laws and corrected their defects from the group of French and British laws, adding to them some Islamic laws for the purpose of camouflage and deception. The provisions in the constitution that define the system of government and that set up the monarchy and the hereditary rule as a system of government for the country are imported from England and Belgium and copied from the constitutions of the European countries. These provisions are alien to Islam and are in conflict with it.

Is there monarchy, hereditary rule or succession to the throne in Islam? How can this happen in Islam when we know that the monarchic rule is in conflict with the Islamic rule and with the Islamic political system? Islam abolished monarchy and succession to the throne. When it first appeared, Islam considered the sultanic systems of rule in Iran, Egypt, Yemen and the (eastern) Roman Empire illegal. God's prophet, may God's prayers be upon him, sent messages to the king of the Romans (Hercules) and the king of 'Persia urging them to set the people free to worship God alone because only God is the sultan. Monarchy and succession to the throne are the ominous and null system of government against which al-Husayn, the master of martyrs, rose and fought. Rejecting injustice and refusing to submit to Yazid's succession and rule, al-Husayn staged his historic revolution and urged all the Moslems to follow suit. There is no hereditary monarchic system in Islam. If they consider this a defect in Islam, then let them say: Islam is defective. Added to this defect is the fact that Islam has failed to organize usury, disregarded alcohol drinking and failed to organize fornication and abomination. To correct these defects and to fill these voids, the ruling authorities— the foster child of colonialism—resorted to legislating laws organizing these matters, adopting such laws from England,

9

France, Belgium and the United States. We know that all this is taboo in our religion and that one of the proud points of our Islam is that it is free of regulations concerning such matters.

At the outset of the so-called constitutional era, the British colonialism exerted efforts aimed at two things: One was to defeat the Russian influence in Iran and the second was to oust and expel Islam from the sphere of application and import Western laws to replace the laws of Islam.

These foreign laws caused the Moslem society numerous problems. Experienced jurists are grumbling about them and whoever is involved in a judiciary or legal case in Iran, or in similar states, must spend a long life to win such a case. A proficient lawyer has told me: I can keep a case between two disputants in the courts all my life and it is most likely that my son will succeed me to the case. This is a fact at present. Excluded from this are the illicit profits that people with influence gain from their cases through trickery, perfidy, bribery, deception and cheating. We find that the present judiciary laws intend for the people nothing but hardship. The case on which the Shari'a judge used to make a decision in two or three days now takes twenty years to settle. During this time, a young man turns old for having to check with the judiciary authorities morning and evening, having to roam their halls hopelessly and for having to be brought back to these authorities and halls whenever he wants to leave them.

They write at times in their books and papers: The penalties of Islam are cruel and harsh. One of them has dared to say with utter impudence: "The harshness of these penalties is derived from the harshness of nomadism. The harshness of the Arabs is what has caused these penalties to be harsh."

I wonder how these people think. They carry out the death sentence, under the pretext of the law, against several people for smuggling ten grams of heroin. I have learned that they

10

executed some time ago ten persons, one after the other, for smuggling ten grams of heroin. When they legislate these inhumane laws under the pretext of preventing corruption, they see no harshness in them. I do not condone dealing in heroin but I oppose death as a penalty for dealing in heroin. Dealing in heroin must be fought but on a basis compatible with the dimensions of the crime.

Punishing an alcohol drinker with eighty whip lashes is harsh but executing people for smuggling ten grams of heroin is not harsh when most forms of social corruption are caused by alcohol! Traffic accidents on the highways, incidents of suicide and even heroin addiction—according to some people—are the consequences of drunkenness and alcohol drinking. Yet, they do not ban alcohol because the West has permitted it. This is why they sell and buy alcohol with utter freedom. Woe to Islam from them!

If an alcohol drinker is to be given eighty lashes or an (unmarried) adulterer is to be punished with one hundred lashes and if a married adulterer or adulteress are to be stoned, you hear them scream: These are cruel and harsh sentences derived from the harshness of the Arabs, whereas the fact is that the provisions of the penal code in Islam came to prevent fornication, abomination and corruption in a big and vast nation. Now we find that corruption has reached the degree where our youths are lost in it because this corruption has been advocated and has been provided with the necessary facilities. If Islam were to intervene at this moment and to punish an alcohol drinker by whipping him in the presence of a group of believers, these people will accuse Islam of cruelty and harshness. On the other hand, no objection must be made against the bloody massacres that have been taking place in Vietnam for fifteen years on the hands of the masters of these rules despite the exorbitant costs that are extorted from the pockets of peoples. If Islam wants to defend itself and to declare war to end corruption, they scream: Why has the war erupted?

Not Gods purpose with Israel the corruption was taking of human life or among Canaanites mutilation

11

All these are plans that were designed and drawn up hundreds of years ago and they are implementing them gradually. At the outset, they established a school somewhere. We did not lift a finger and we, and people like us, failed to prevent this. These schools increased gradually and now you find that they have advocates in all the villages. They have worked to lead our children away from their religion. Some of their plans are represented in keeping us as we are—backward, weak and miserable—so that they may benefit from our resources, our minerals, our lands and our manpower. They believe that we must remain miserable and poor and with no knowledge of what Islam has legislated for dealing with poverty so that they, their agents and their lackeys may live in palaces and towers and enjoy a soft and luxurious life. Their plans have left their impact even on our religious and scientific academies to the degree where if somebody wants to talk on the issue of the Islamic government, he must resort to dissimulation or face the agents of colonialism; and to the degree that when the first edition of this book was published, it enraged the Shah's agents in Iraq and exposed their character through the desperate moves that they made—moves that did them no good.

Yes, our situation has reached the degree where some of us consider the apparel of war and combat incompatible with manliness and with justice whereas our imams put on for war its apparel and took for it its machines and whereas they waged wars. 'Ali, the amir of the faithful, used to put on the war apparel and carry a sword which had its own litter and so did al-Hasan and al-Husayn. Had the opportunity risen, Imam Muhammad al-Baqir would have followed suit afterward. How can wearing the apparel of war be incompatible with social justice and manliness when we want to form an Islamic government? Has what we want been achieved with the turban and the cloak, considering that anything else is incompatible with valor and justice?

What we are suffering from currently is the consequence of that misleading propaganda whose perpetrators got what

12

they wanted and which has required us to exert a large effort to prove that Islam contains principles and rules for the formation of government.

This is our situation. The enemies have implanted these falsehoods in the minds of people in cooperation with their agents, have ousted Islam's judiciary and political laws from the sphere of application and have replaced them by European laws in contempt of Islam for the purpose of driving it away from society. They have exploited every available opportunity for this end.

These are the destructive plans of colonialism. If we add to them the internal elements of weakness among some of our people, we find that the result is that people begin to grow smaller and to despise themselves in the face of the material progress of the enemies. When some states advance industrially and scientifically, some of us grow smaller and begin to think that our failure to do the same is due to our religion and that the only means to achieve such progress is to abandon religion and its laws and to violate the Islamic teachings and beliefs. When the enemies went to the moon, these people imagined that religion was the obstacle preventing them from doing the same! I would like to tell these people: The laws of the Eastern or the Western camps are not what led them to this magnificent advance in invading outer space. The laws of these two camps are totally different. Let them go to Mars or anywhere they wish; they are still backward in the sphere of securing happiness to man, backward in spreading moral virtues and backward in creating a psychological and spiritual progress similar to the material progress. They are still unable to solve their social problems because solving these problems and eliminating hardship requires an ideological and moral spirit. The material gains in the sphere of overcoming nature and invading space cannot accomplish this task. Wealth, capabilities and resources require the Islamic faith, creed and ethics to become complete and balanced, to serve man and to avert from him injustice and poverty. We alone possess such

13

morals and laws. Therefore, we should not cast aside our religion and our laws, which are directly connected with man's life and which harbor the nucleus of reforming people and securing their happiness in this world and in the hereafter, as soon as we see somebody go to the moon or make something.

The ideas disseminated by the colonialists among us include their statement: "There is no government in the Islamic legislation and there are no govermnent organizations in Islam. Assuming that there are important Shari'a laws, these laws lack the elements to guarantee their implementation. Consequently, Islam is a legislator and nothing more." It is evident that such statements are an indivisible part of the colonialist plans that seek to divert the Moslems away from thinking of politics, government and administration. These statements are in conflict with our primary beliefs. We believe in government and we believe in the need for the prophet to appoint a caliph (successor) after him, and he did. What does the appointment of a successor mean? Does it mean a mere explanation of the laws? The mere explaining of laws does not require a successor. It would have been enough for the prophet, God's prayers be upon him, to disseminate the laws among the people and then lodge them in a book and leave it with the people to consult after him. The need for a successor is for the implementation of the laws because no law without an executor is respected. In the entire world, legislation alone is not enough and cannot secure the happiness of people. There must be an executive authority and the absence of such an authority in any nation is a factor of deficiency and weakness. This is why Islam decided to establish an executive power to implement God's laws. The person in charge is the one who implements the laws. This is what the prophet, may God's prayers be upon him, did. Had he not done so, he would not have conveyed his message. The appointment of a successor after him to implement and uphold the laws and to spread justice among the people was an element complementing and completing the prophet's message. In his days, the prophet, may God's

14

prayers be upon him, was not content with explaining and conveying the laws. He also implemented them. God's prophet, may God's prayers be upon him, was the executor of the law. He punished, cut off the thief's hand, lashed and stoned and ruled justly. A successor is needed for such acts. A successor is not the conveyor of laws and not a legislator. A successor is needed for implementation. Here is where the importance of forming government and of creating and organizing executive agencies emerges. The belief in the need for forming government and for creating such agencies is an indivisible part of the belief in governance. Exerting efforts for and seeking this goal are an aspect of the belief in governance.

You must show Islam as it should be shown. Define governance to the people as it is. Tell them: We believe in governance; that the prophet, God's prayers be upon him, appointed a successor on the orders of God; we believe in the need for forming government; and we seek to implement God's order and rule to manage people, run their affairs and care for them. The struggle for forming government is a twin to the faith in governance. Write and disseminate the laws of Islam and do not conceal them. Pledge to apply an Islamic rule, rely on yourselves and be confident of victory.

The colonialists prepared themselves more than three centuries ago and started from the zero point. They have gotten what they wanted. Let us now start from scratch. Do not allow the Westerners and their followers to dominate you. Familiarize the people with the truth of Islam so that the young generation may not think that the men of religion in the mosques of Qum and al-Najaf believe in the separation of church from state, that they study nothing other than menstruation and childbirth and that they have nothing to do with politics. The colonialists have spread in school curricula the need to separate church from the state and have deluded people into believing that the ulema of Islam are not qualified to interfere in the political and social

15

affairs. The lackeys and followers of the colonialists have reiterated these words. In the prophet's time, was the church separated from the state? Were there at the time theologians and politicians? At the time of the caliphs and the time of 'Ali, the amir of the faithful, was the state separated from the church? Was there an agency for the church and another for the state?

The colonialists and their lackeys have made these statements to isolate religion from the affairs of life and society and to tacitly keep the ulema of Islam away from the people and drive people away from the ulema because the ulema struggle for the liberation and independence of the Moslems. When their wish of separation and isolation is realized, the colonialists and their lackeys can take away our resources and rule us. I tell you that if our sole concern is to pray, to implore and mention God and never go beyond, colonialism and all the agencies of aggression will never oppose us. Pray as you wish and call for prayer as you wish and let them take what God has given you. The final account is to God and God is the only source of strength and might. When we die our reward will come from God—if this is our thinking, then we have nothing to be concerned with or to fear.

It has been said that a commander of the British occupation of Iraq heard a muezzin call for prayers and asked about the harm that such a call causes the British policy. When he was told that there was no harm, the commander said: Let him say whatever he wants as long as he does not criticize us. If you do not deal with the colonialist policy and if your study of the laws does not go beyond the theological framework, they will not bother you. Pray as you wish. They want your oil, so what do they care about your prayers. They want our minerals, and they want to open our markets for their goods and capital. This is why we find the lackey governments obstruct the industrialization of the country, being content at times with assembly plants and nothing else. They do not want to rise to the level of human beings because they fear the human beings. If they find a human being somewhere,

16

they are terrified by him because this human being is progressive and advanced and can influence people and society in a manner that destroys all that the enemy has built and that shakes the earth under the thrones of tyranny, treason and lackeyhood. This is why when they see a human being at any time, they plot against him to kill him, to fix him (yuthabbituhu), to oust him or to accuse him of being a politician. This clergyman is a politician! But was not the prophet, God's prayers be upon him, a politician? Is there anything shameful in being a politician? All these things are said by the enemy's agents and lackeys to keep you away from politics and from society's affairs and to prevent you from fighting the authorities of treason and tyranny so that they may have a free hand, may do what they like and may plunder whatever they want without any opposition or any obstruction.

PROOF OF NEED FOR FORMING GOVERNMENT

Need for Executive Agencies

A collection of laws is not enough to reform society. For a law to be an element for reforming and making people happy, it requires an executive authority. This is why God, may He be praised, created on earth, in addition to the laws, a government and an executive and administrative agency. The great prophet, may God's prayers be upon him, headed all the executive agencies running the Moslem society. In addition to the tasks of conveying, explaining and detailing the laws and the regulations, he took care of implementing them until he brought the State of Islam into existence. In his time, the prophet was not content with legislating the penal code, for example, but also sought to implement it. He cut off hands, whipped and stoned. After the prophet, the

17

tasks of the caliph were no less than those of the prophet. The appointment of a caliph was not for the sole purpose of explaining the laws but also for implementing them. This is the goal that endowed the caliphate with importance and significance. The prophet, had he not appointed a caliph to succeed him, would have been considered to have failed to convey his message. The Moslems were new to Islam and were in direct need for somebody to implement the laws and to make God's will and orders the judge among people to secure their happiness in this world and in the hereafter.

In truth, the social laws and regulations need an executor. In all countries of the world, legislation alone is not enough and cannot secure people's happiness. The legislative authority must be followed by an executive authority which is the only authority that can bring to people the fruits of just legislation. This is why Islam decided to establish an executive authority side by side with the legislative authority and appointed a person in charge to implement, in addition to teaching, disseminating and explaining.*

Methods of Great Prophet, May God's Prayers Be Upon Him

We learn from the prophet's doings and sayings and from his conduct that it is necessary to form government: First, because he himself formed a government. History attests to this. The prophet assumed the leadership in managing society. He appointed rulers for the provinces, acted as a

* The Koranic verse "O you believers, obey God, obey the prophet and obey those in charge among you" requires us to obey those in charge. The people in charge after the prophet are the imams who have been entrusted with explaining the Islamic laws and rules and with disseminating them among the Moslems and other peoples of the world. The imams have also been entrusted with implementing these laws and rules. The just jurisprudents have been required to carry out these tasks after the imams.

judge to settle the disputes among people and sent ambassadors outside the borders of his state, to the chiefs of tribes and to kings. He concluded treaties and he led wars. Consequently, he implemented all the laws of Islam.

Second: He appointed, on orders from God, a successor to carry out these tasks after him. This appointment of a successor indicates clearly the need for the government after the prophet to continue. Considering that this appointment of a successor was on orders from God, then the continuation of government and of its agencies and organizations is also ordered by God.

Need for Continued Implementation of Laws

It is obvious that the need for implementing the laws was not exclusive to the prophet's age and that this need continues because Islam is not limited by time or place. Because Islam is immortal, it must be implemented and observed forever. If what was permissible by Muhammad is permissible until the day of resurrection and what was forbidden by Muhammad is forbidden to the day of resurrection, then Muhammad's restrictions must not be suspended, his teachings must not be neglected, punishment must not be abandoned, tax collection must not be stopped and defense of the nation of the Moslems and of their lands must not be abandoned. The beliefs that Islam came for a limited period and for a certain place violates the essentials of the Islamic beliefs. Considering that the implementation forever of laws after the venerable prophet, may God's prayers be upon him, is one of the essentials of life, then it is necessary for government to exist and for this government to have the qualities of an executive and administrative authority. Without this, social chaos, corruption and ideological and moral deviation would prevail. This can be prevented only through the creation of a just government that runs all aspects of life.

In Time of Amir of Faithful ('Ali ibn Abi Talib)

No Moslem doubted the need for the continued presence of the government after the prophet, may God's prayers be upon him. All agreed on this. The disagreement was on who was to be in charge. The government was present after the prophet, especially in the time of 'Ali, the amir of the faithful, with all its administrative and executive agencies. There is no doubt about this.

Truth of Islamic Laws

The nature of the Islamic laws is another proof of the need for forming government. They show us that they came for the formation of government with an administration, with a sound economy and with a high culture.

First, provisions of the Islamic canonical law contain various laws for a complete social system. Under this system, all of man's needs are met, beginning with the relationships of neighborliness, of children and tribe and with fellow citizens, with all aspects of family and married life and ending with legislations concerning war and peace, international relations, penal laws, commercial, industrial and agricultural rights. The canonical law also regulates legal matrimony and what the couple eats when married and in the period of nursing. Islam regulates the duties of the parents who are entrusted with bringing up the children, the relationship of husband with wife and wife with husband and the relationship of each of them with the children. In all these spheres, Islam has laws and regulations to raise perfect and virtuous human beings. Islam promulgates the law, keeps it alive, implements it and works intrinsically for it. It is well known to what degree Islam has devoted attention to society's political and economic relations so as to create a polished and virtuous human being.

The venerable Koran and the noble Sunna contain all the rules and regulations to make human beings happy and to lead them toward perfection.

Al-Kafi's book contains a chapter entitled: "Explanation of All That People Need in the Book and the Sunna." The book explains everything. The imam (al-Kafi) swears, according to some Hadiths, that all that people need is undoubtedly found in the book and the Sunna.

Second, when we examine the nature of the provisions of the canonical law closely, it becomes certain to us that it is impossible to implement them except through a government with capable agencies. I will give you a few examples and the faithful brothers will have to explore the rest:

1. Financial Laws

The financial taxes legislated by Islam do not contain anything to indicate that they were legislated to feed the poor, expecially the sadahs (direct descendants of Muhammad) among them. They indicate that their legislation was for the purpose of securing the expenditures of a major sovereign state.

For example, the one-fifth tax is an enormous source of income that yields to the treasury enormous sums of money that constitute the larger part of this treasury. In our creed, one-fifth is collected for all gains, benefits and profits, whether from agriculture, commerce, minerals or treasures. A vegetable vendor participates in paying the one-fifth tax if he earns that which is in excess of his annual supply needs, as specified by the teachings of the Shari'a on expenditure and spending. A ship's captain and a prospector for minerals and treasures also participate and pay to the imam or the

21

Moslem ruler one-fifth of the surplus profits so that he may turn them over to the treasury house. It is obvious that this enormous resource is for the purpose of managing the affairs of the Moslem state and of meeting all its needs. If we were to calculate the one-fifth of the profits of the Moslem State or of the entire world, if it were Moslem, it would become obvious to us that these enormous funds are not for the purpose of meeting the needs of a sayyid (direct descendant of prophet) or of an education seeker but for a greater and broader purpose, i. e., for meeting the needs of an entire nation. When a Moslem state is established, then such a state must use the help of the one-fifth tax, of the alms tax, the tax on non-Moslems* and land tax.

When have the direct descendants of the prophet been in need of such money? The one-fifth tax collected from the Baghdad market is enough for the needs of all these descendants, for the expenses of all the theological academies and for all the poor Moslems, not to mention the markets of Teheran, Islampol (Constantinople), Cairo and other markets. Such an enormous budget is intended for running the affairs of a major nation, for meeting the important essential needs of people and for providing the public health, educational, cultural, defense and construction needs.

The coordination required by Islam in collecting, safeguarding and spending funds guarantees freedom of the public treasury from injustice and unfairness. The treasury does not belong to the head of state, to the officials or to the government members. Any privileges may be misused. The nation's treasury is for all the people alike.

* This is a tax collected annually from the followers of the book, namely the Jews and the Christians. These people live under the protection of the Moslem State and are exempted from the one-fifth tax and the alms tax. They are also exempted from carrying arms to defend the Moslem state. They benefit from the state agencies in the same manner as Moslems do.

Should we throw this enormous wealth into the sea? Should we bury it in the ground until al-Hijjah (awaited leader of Shi'ites) comes or should we distribute it to 50 or 500,000 Hashimites? If this money is given to them, would not they be astounded and amazed? Don't we know that the right of the Hashimites to this money goes only to the degree of what they need to spend purposely and moderately? All that there is to the matter is that the Hashimites should take only their need and nothing more of the one-fifth tax. The Hadith says that these people should return to the imam what exceeds the needs of their year and that the imam should help them when what they take from the treasury house is not enough for their annual needs.

If we examine the monies collected through the tax imposed on the followers of the Book (Christians and Jews) and through the land tax, we would find that there is an enormous wealth that cannot be taken lightly. The ruler or the person in charge must impose on the followers of the book a tax compatible with their financial capability. He must also impose land tax on lands utilized under the supervision of the state and this tax must be deposited in the treasury house. All this requires the formation of special agencies, careful accounts, management and records and foresight so that there may be no chaos. All this indicates clearly the need to form government because these legislations cannot be realized practically until after completing and stabilizing the government formations.

2. *Defense Laws*

On the other hand, we find that the laws governing struggle and defense of the Moslems to secure the nation's independence and dignity also indicate the need for forming government.

Islam has dictated the need for preparing and being fully ready and alert, even in peace time, according to His words, may He be praised: "Prepare for them all the force and the horses you can muster so that you may scare away the enemies of God and your enemies." Had the Moslems adhered to the meaning of this Koranic phrase and had they been ready to fight under all circumstances, it would not have been possible for a handful of Jews to occupy our land and to damage and burn our al-Aqsa Mosque without being faced with any resistance. All this came about as an inevitable result of the failure of the Moslems to carry out God's instruction and their failure to form an upright and faithful government. Had the current Moslem rulers tried to implement the laws of Islam, abandoning all their differences, putting aside their disputes and their division and uniting in one hand in the face of the others, the bands of Jews and the puppets of America and Britain would not have been able to reach what they have reached, regardless of how much America and Britain help them. The reason for this is, of course, the fact that the Moslem rulers are unfit and unqualified.

The phrase "prepare for them all the force you can muster...." orders that we be fully prepared and alert so that the enemies may not subject us to the worst forms of torture. But we did not unite, we split into factions, our hearts were disunited and we did not get ready and so the unjust went beyond all limits in tyrannizing us and inflicting injustice upon us.

3. Laws on Strictures, Blood Money, and Penalties

These laws cannot be established without government authorities. Through these authorities, blood money is collected from the culprit and paid to the victim, restrictions are established and punishment is placed under the supervision and control of the religious ruler.

NEED FOR POLITICAL REVOLUTION

At the early stage of Islam, the Ommiads and those supporting them tried to obstruct the stability of the government of Imam 'Ali ibn Abi Talib, even though it was a government that pleased God and the prophet. With their hateful efforts, the method and system of government changed and deviated from Islam because the programs of the Ommiads were in complete conflict with the teachings of Islam. The Abbasides came after the Ommiads and followed the same path. The caliphate changed and turned into a sultanate and a hereditary monarchy. The rule became similar to that of the emperors of Persia and Rome and the pharaohs of Egypt. This situation has continued until our present day.

The Shari'a and reason require us not to let governments have a free hand. The proof of this is evident. The persistence of these governments in their transgressions means obstructing the system and laws of Islam whereas there are numerous provisions that describe every non-Islamic system as a form of idolatry and a ruler or an authority in such a system as a false god. We are responsible for eliminating the traces of idolatry from our Moslem society and for keeping it away from our life. At the same time, we are responsible for preparing the right atmosphere for bringing up a faithful generation that destroys the thrones of false gods and destroys their illegal powers because corruption and deviation grow on their hands. This corruption must be wiped out and erased and the severest punishment must be inflicted upon those who cause it. In His venerable book, God describes Pharaoh as "a corrupter." Under the canopy of a pharonic rule that dominates and corrupts society rather than reform it, no faithful and pious person can live abiding by and preserving his faith and piety. Such a person has before him two paths, and no third to them: either be forced to commit sinful acts or rebel against and fight the rule of false gods, try to wipe out or at least reduce the impact of such a rule. We only have the second path open to us. We have no alternative but to work for destroying the corrupt and corrupting systems and to destroy the symbol of treason and the unjust among the rulers of peoples.

This is a duty that all Moslems wherever they may be are entrusted—a duty to create a victorious and triumphant Islamic political revolution.

Need for Islamic Unity

On the other hand, colonialism has partitioned our home-land and has turned the Moslems into peoples. When the Ottoman State appeared as a united state, the colonialists sought to fragment it. The Russians, the British and their allies united and fought the Ottomans and then shared the loot, as you all know. We do not deny that most rulers of the Ottoman State lacked ability, competence and qualifica-tions and many of them ruled the people in a despotic monarchic manner. However, the colonialists were afraid that some pious and qualified persons would, with the help of the people, assume leadership of the Ottoman State and (would safeguard) its unity, ability, strength and resources, thus dispersing the hopes and aspirations of the colonialists. This is why as soon as World War I ended, the colonialists partitioned the country into mini-states and made each of these mini-states their agent. Despite this, a number of these mini-states later escaped the grip of colonialism and its agents.

The only means that we possess to unite the Moslem nation, to liberate its lands from the grip of the colonialists and to topple the agent governments of colonialism, is to seek to establish our Islamic government. The efforts of this govern-ment will be crowned with success when we become able to destroy the heads of treason, the idols, the human images and the false gods who disseminate injustice and corruption on earth.

The formation of a government is then for the purpose of preserving the unity of the Moslems after it is achieved. This was mentioned in the speech of Fatimah al-Zahra', may peace be upon her, when she said: ". . . In obeying us lies the nation's order, and our imamhood is a guarantee against division."

Need for Rescuing Wronged and Deprived

To achieve their unjust economic goals, the colonialists employed the help of their agents in our countries. As a result of this, there are hundreds of millions of starving people who lack the simplest health and educational means. On the other side, there are individuals with excessive wealth and broad corruption. The starving people are in a constant struggle to improve their conditions and to free themselves from the tyranny of the aggressive rulers. But the ruling minorities and their government agencies are also seeking to extinguish this struggle. On our part, we are entrusted to rescue the deprived and the wronged. We are instructed to help the wronged and to fight the oppressors, as the amir of the faithful ('Ali) instructed his two sons in his will: "Fight the tyrant and aid the wronged."

The Moslem ulema are entrusted to fight the greedy exploiters so that society may not have a deprived beggar and, on the other side, someone living in comfort and luxury and suffering from gluttony. The amir of the faithful ('Ali) says: "By Him Who split the seed and created the breeze, were it not for the presence of the Omnipresent, the presence of the proof of the existence of the Victory Giver, and were it not for God's instructions to the ulema not to condone the oppression of a tyrant nor the suffering of the wronged, I would let matters go unchecked and would get the end mixed up with the beginning and you would find this world of yours less significant to me than a goat's sneeze." *

How can we stand nowadays to keep silent on a handful of exploiters and foreigners who dominate with the force of arms when these people have denied hundreds of millions of others the joy of enjoying the smallest degree of life's pleasures and blessings? The duty of the ulema and of all the Moslems is to put an end to this injustice and to seek to bring happiness to millions of peoples through destroying and eliminating the unjust governments and through establishing a sincere and active Moslem government.

Need for Formation of Government in Hadith

This need has already been proven by the dictates of reason and of the Shari'a, by the prophet's life and by the life of the amir of the faithful and through the meaning of many Koranic phrases and Hadiths. As an example of this need, we will cite the saying of Imam al-Rida:

"'Abd-al-Wahid ibn Muhammad ibn 'Abdus al-Nisaburi al-'Attar said: Abu-al-Hasan 'Ali ibn Muhammad ibn Qutay-bah al-Nisaburi said: Abu Muhammad al-Fadl ibn Shadhan al-Nisaburi said: If somebody asks: Tell me, is it possible that the Wise appoints (rulers) and if somebody asks: Why did He appoint people in charge and order that they be obeyed? The answer is: For many reasons, one of them the fact that people have been ordered to observe certain strictures and not to violate them, because violating the restrictions corrupts people. This could not be established and realized without appointing a trustee over the people to stop them at what they are permitted and to prevent them from violating what is banned to them. Without this,

* Nahj al-Balaghahj, 1/41

28

nobody would abandon his benefit and pleasure so that he may not corrupt others—this is what the copy says whereas the correct version is: Nobody would abandon his pleasure. The reasons also include the fact that we find no faction and no nation that lived and survived without a trustee and leader to manage their inevitable religious and secular affairs. In His wisdom, God would not leave the people without that which he knows they must have and without which they cannot survive, that with which to fight their enemy, to divide their rewards, to unite them and to deter the unjust among them from doing others an injustice. The reasons also include the fact that if He did not appoint for people an imam, trustee, preserver and pacifier, the nation would be obliterated, religion would disappear, laws and rules would be changed and the heretics would add to them and the atheists would detract from them and would have attributed this to the Moslems because we have found people to be deficient and imperfect, regardless of their inclinations and their various states. Had He not set up a trustee and a preserver, the first prophet would not have appointed one and people would have degenerated as we have demonstrated, laws, rules and faith would have changed and this would have led to the corruption of all mankind."

You can see that Imam al-Rida cites several aspects as proof of the need for the presence of a person in charge to govern people. The reasons that he mentioned are present at all times. Consequently it is necessary to form the Islamic government at all times because violating the restrictions of God, seeking personal pleasure, spreading corruption on earth and disregarding the rights of the weak are things that are present at all times and are not confined to a specific time. This is why the Divine Wisdom dictated that people live justly within the restrictions imposed upon them by God. This Wisdom is constant and everlasting. Therefore, the presence of a person in charge of the Islamic laws and rules is essential because such a presence prevents injustice, violation and corruption and because this person carries the trust, guides people to the straight path and thwarts the heresies of the atheists and of the pertinacious. Wasn't the caliphate given to the amir of the faithful for this purpose? These reasons and needs that made Imam 'Ali take charge of the people are present currently, with one difference, namely that the imam is spelled out specifically as the man in charge whereas in our days the person of the religious ruler has been defined through defining his identity, qualities and qualifications in a general manner.

If we want to immortalize the rules of the Shari'a in practice, to prevent violation of the rights of weak people, to prevent corruption on earth, to apply the Shari'a laws justly, to fight the heresies and the deviations decided upon by the rigged up—parliamentary—councils and to prevent the influence and intervention of the enemies in the affairs of the Moslems, we must form the government, because all this is carried out by a government led by a trustworthy and pious ruler who commits no injustice, deviation or corruption.

Previously, we did not work and did not rise together to form a government to destroy all the traitors and corrupters. Some of us have displayed lukewarmness even in the theoretical sphere and have failed to call for Islam and for spreading its laws. Perhaps some of us have been preoccupied with imploring God for these things. As a result, all these conditions have come into existence: The influence of the Islamic law in the Moslem society has diminished; the nation has been afflicted with division, weakness and degeneration; the rules of Islam have been obstructed; and the situation has changed. The colonialists have used all this as an easy opportunity, brought foreign laws to which God has given no power, spread their poisoned cultures and thoughts and disseminated them among the Moslems, and we have lost the formations of the proper government. All this is obvious.

ISLAMIC SYSTEM OF GOVERNMENT

Distinction from Other Political Systems

The Islamic government is not similar to the well-known systems of government. It is not a despotic government in which the head of state dictates his opinion and tampers with the lives and property of the people. The prophet, may God's prayers be upon him, and 'Ali, the amir of the faithful, and the other imams had no power to tamper with people's property or with their lives. The Islamic government is not despotic but constitutional. However, it is not constitutional in the well-known sense of the word, which is represented in the parliamentary system or in the people's councils. It is constitutional in the sense that those in charge of affairs observe a number of conditions and rules underlined in the Koran and in the Sunna and represented in the necessity of observing the system and of applying the dictates and laws of Islam. This is why the Islamic government is the government of the divine law. The difference between the Islamic government and the constitutional governments, both monarchic and republican, lies in the fact that the people's representatives or the king's representatives are the ones who codify and legislate, whereas the power of legislation is confined to God, may He be praised, and nobody else has the right to legislate and nobody may rule by that which has not been given power by God. This is why Islam replaces the legislative council* by a planning council that works to run the affairs and work of the ministries so that they may offer their services in all spheres.

*The legislative council is one of three powers in all states in modern ages. These are the legislative power, the judiciary power and the executive power (cabinet).

31

All that is mentioned in the book (Koran) and in the Sunna is acceptable and obeyed in the view of the Moslems. This obedience facilitates the state's responsibilities, however when the majorities in the constitutional monarchic or republican governments legislate something, the government has to later exert efforts to compel people to obey, even if such obedience requires the use of force.

The Islamic government is the government of the law and God alone is the ruler and the legislator. God's rule is effective among all the people and in the state itself. All individuals—the prophet, his successors and other people—follow what Islam, which descended through revelation and which God has explained through the Koran and through the words of His prophet, has legislated for them.

The venerable prophet, may God's peace and prayers be upon him, was appointed ruler on earth by God so that he may rule justly and not follow whims. God addressed the prophet through revelation and told him to convey what was revealed to him to those who would succeed him. The prophet obeyed the dictates of this order and appointed 'Ali, the amir of the faithful, as his successor. He was not motivated in this appointment by the fact that 'Ali was his son-in-law and the fact that 'Ali had performed weighty and unforgettable services but because God ordered the prophet to do so.

Yes, government in Islam means obeying the law and making it the judge. The powers given to the prophet, may God's peace and prayers be upon him, and to the legitimate rulers after him are powers derived from God. God ordered that the prophet and the rulers after him be obeyed: "Obey the prophet and those in charge among you." There is no place for opinions and whims in the government of Islam. The prophet, the imams and the people obey God's will and Shari'a.

The government of Islam is not monarchic, not a shahin-shahdom and not an empire, because Islam is above squandering and unjustly undermining the lives and property of people. This is why the government of Islam does not have the many big palaces, the servants, the royal courts, the crown prince courts and other trivial requirements that consume half or most of the country's resources and that the sultans and the emperors have. The life of the great prophet was a life of utter simplicity, even though the prophet was the head of the state, who ran and ruled it by himself. This method continued to a degree after him and until the Ommiads seized power. The government of 'Ali ibn Abi Talib was a government of reform, as you know, and 'Ali lived a life of utter simplicity while managing a vast state in which Iran, Egypt, Hejaz and Yemen were mere provinces under his rule. I do not believe that any of our poor people can live the kind of life that the imam ('Ali) lived. When he had two cloaks, he gave the better one to Qanbar, his servant, and he wore the other. When he found extra material in his sleeves, he cut it off. Had this course continued until the present, people would have known the taste of happiness and the country's treasury would not have been plundered to be spent on fornication, abomination and the court's costs and expenditures. You know that most of the corrupt aspects of our society are due to the corruption of the ruling dynasty and the royal family. What is the legitimacy of these rulers who build houses of entertainment, corruption, fornication and abomination and who destroy houses which God ordered be raised and in which His name is mentioned? Were it not for what the court wastes and what it embezzles, the country's budget would not experience any deficit that forces the state to borrow from America and England, with all the humiliation and insult that accompany such borrowing. Has our oil decreased or have our minerals that are stored under this good earth run out? We possess everything and we would not need the help of America or of others if it were not for the costs of the court and for its wasteful use of the people's money. This is on the one hand. On the other hand, there are state agencies that are not

33

needed and that consume money, resources, paper and equipment. This is a waste banned by our religion because such waste escalates the people's problems, wastes their time and effort and consumes monies of which they are in the direct need. In Islam, when Islam was the ruler, justice was dispensed, restrictions established and disputes settled with utter simplicity. The qadi (judge) saw to it that all this was done by a handful of persons with some pencils and a little ink and paper. Behind all this, the qadi directed people to work for an honorable and virtuous life. But now, only God knows the number of the justice departments, bureaus and employees—all of which are futile and do the people no good, not to mention the hardship, difficulties, waste of time and monies, and, consequently, the loss of justice and rights that they cause the people.

Qualifications of Ruler

The qualifications that must be available to the ruler emanate from the nature of the Islamic government. Regardless of the general qualifications, such as intelligence, maturity and a good sense of management, there are two important qualifications:

1. Knowledge of Islamic Law

2. Justice

A. In view of the fact that the Islamic government is a government of law, it is a must that the ruler of the Moslems be knowledgeable in the law, as the Hadith says. Whoever occupies a (public) post or carries out a certain task must know as much as he needs within the limits of his jurisdiction and the ruler must know more than everybody else. Our imams proved their worthiness of the people's trust by their early search for knowledge. What the Shiite ulema fault others for revolves mostly around the level of knowledge attained by our ulema—a standard that the others failed to rise to.

Knowledge of the law and of justice are among the most important mainstays of the imamate. If a person knows a lot about nature and its secrets and masters many arts but is ignorant of the law, then his knowledge does not qualify him for the caliphate and does not put him ahead of those who know the law and deal with justice. It is an acknowledged fact among the Moslems since the first days and until our persent day that the ruler or the caliph must know the law and possess the faculty of justice with a sound faith and good ethics. This is what sound reason requires, especially since we know that the Islamic government is an actual embodiment of the law and not a matter of whims. A person ignorant of the laws is not qualified to rule because if he imitates in his decisions; his rule will have no dignity, and if he does not imitate, he will be unable to carry out the laws, assuming he is totally ignorant of the laws. It is an acknowledged fact that "the jurisprudents are rulers over the kings." If the sultans are somewhat religious, then all they have to do is proceed in their decisions and actions on the advice of jurisprudents. In such a case, the real rulers are the jurisprudents, and the sultans are nothing but people working for them.

Naturally, it is not the duty of any civil servant whatever his task to know all the laws and to study them deeply. It is enough for such a person to familiarize himself with the laws of importance to his work or to the task entrusted to him. This is how matters proceeded in the time of the prophet and of the amir of the faithful. The supreme ruler knows all the Islamic laws, and the emissaries, envoys, workers and provincial rulers are content to know the laws and legislation pertaining to their tasks and refer to the sources of legislation designated for them of matters that they do not know.

B. The ruler must have the highest degree of faith in the creed, good ethics, the sense of justice and freedom from sins, because whoever undertakes to set the strictures, to achieve the rights, and to organize the revenues and expenditures of the treasury house must not be unjust. God says in his precious book: "The unjust shall not have my support." Thus, if the ruler is not just, he cannot be trusted not to betray the trust and not to favor himself, his family and his relatives over the people.

The opinion of the Shi'a who is entitled to lead the people is known since the death of the prophet and until the time of the disappearance (of the Shiite leader). To the Shi'a, the imam is a virtuous man who knows the laws and implements them justly and who fears nobody's censure in serving God.

Ruler in Time of Absence

If we believe that the laws concerning the establishment of the Islamic government are still present and that the Shari'a denounces chaos, then we must form the government. Reason dictates that this is necessary, especially if an enemy surprises us or if an aggressor who must be fought and repelled attacks us. The Shari'a has ordered us to prepare for them all the force that we can muster to scare God's enemy and our enemy, and it encourages us to retaliate against those who attack us with whatever they attack us. Islam also calls for doing the wronged justice, for wrenching his rights and for deterring the unjust. All this requires strong agencies. As for the expenses of the government that is to be formed for the service of the people—the entire people— these expenses come from the treasury house, whose revenues consist of the land tax, the one-fifth tax and the tax levied on Jews and Christians and other resources.

Now, in the time of absence, there is no provision for a certain person to manage the state affairs. So what is the opinion? Should we allow the laws of Islam to continue to be idle? Do we persuade ourselves to turn away from Islam or do we say that Islam came to rule people for a couple of centuries and then to neglect them? Or do we say that Islam has neglected to organize the state? We know that the absence of the government means the loss and violation of the bastions of the Moslems and means our failure to gain our right and our land. Is this permitted in our religion? Isn't the government one of the necessities of life? Despite the absence of a provision designating an individual to act on behalf of the imam ('Ali) in the case of his absence, the presence of the qualities of the religious ruler in any individual still qualify him to rule the people. These qualities, which are knowledge of the law and justice, are available in most of our jurisprudents in this age. If they decide, it will be easy for them to create and establish a just government unequalled in the world.

Rule of Jurisprudent

If a knowledgeable and just jurisprudent undertakes the task of forming the government, then he will run the social affairs that the prophet used to run and it is the duty of the people to listen to him and obey him.

This ruler will have as much control over running the people's administration, welfare and policy as the prophet and amir of the faithful had despite the special virtues and the traits that distinguished the prophet and the imam. Their virtues did not entitle them to contradict the instructions of the Shari'a or to dominate people with disregard to God's order. God has given the actual Islamic government that is supposed to be formed in the time of absence (of caliph 'Ali ibn Abi Talib) the same powers that he gave the prophet and the amir of the faithful in regard to ruling, justice and the settlement of disputes, the appointment of provincial rulers and officers, the collection of taxes and the development of

37

the country. All that there is to the matter is that the appointment of the ruler at present depends on (finding) someone who has both knowledge and justice.

Subjective Rule

The above-mentioned must not be misunderstood and nobody should imagine that the fitness of the jurisprudent for rule raises him to the status of prophesy or of imams because our discussion here is not concerned with status and rank but with the actual task. The rule here means governing the people, running the state and applying the laws of the Shari'a. This is a hard task under which those qualified for it buckle without being raised above the level of men. In other words, rule means the government, the administration and the country's policy and not, as some people imagine, a privilege or a favor. It is a practical task of extreme significance.

The rule of the jurisprudent is a subjective matter dictated by the Shari'a, as the Shari'a considers one of us a trustee over minors. The task of a trustee over an entire people is not different from that of the trustee over minors, except quantitatively. If we assume that the prophet and the imam had been trustees over minors, their task in this respect would not have been very different quantitatively and qualitatively from the task of any ordinary person designated as a trustee over those same minors. Their trusteeship over the entire nation is not different practically from the trusteeship of any knowledgeable and just jurisprudent in the time of absence.

If a just jurisprudent capable of establishing the restrictions is appointed, would he establish the restrictions in a manner different from that in which they were established in the days of the prophet or of the amir of the faithful? Did the prophet punish the unmarried fornicator more than one hundred lashes? Does the jurisprudent have to reduce the number to prove that there is a difference between him and the prophet? No, because the ruler, be he a prophet, an imam or a just jurisprudent, is nothing but an executor of God's order and will.

The prophet collected taxes: The one-fifth tax, the alms tax, the tax on the Christians and the Jews and the land tax. Is there a difference between what the prophet and the imam collected and what the present-day jurisprudent should collect?

God made the prophet the ruler of all the faithful and his rule included even the individual who was to succeed him. After the prophet, the imam became the ruler. The significance of their rule is that their legal orders applied to all and that the appointment of, control over and, when necessary, dismissal of judges and provincial rulers was in their hands.

The jurisprudent has this same rule and governance with one difference—namely that the rule of the jurisprudent over other jurisprudents is not so that he can dismiss them because the jurisprudents in the state are equal in terms of competence.

Therefore, the jurisprudents must work separately or collectively to set up a legitimate government that establishes the strictures, protects the borders and establishes order. If competence for this task is confined to one person, then this would be his duty to do so corporeally, otherwise the duty is shared equally. In case it is impossible to form that government, the rule does not disappear.

The jurisprudents have been appointed by God to rule and the jurisprudent must act as much as possible in accordance with his assignment. He must collect the alms tax, the one-fifth tax, the land tax and the tax from Christians and Jews, if he can, so that he may spend all this in the interest of the Moslems. If he can, he must implement the divine strictures. The temporary inability to form a strong and complete government does not at all mean that we should retreat. Dealing with the needs of the Moslems and implementing among them whatever laws are possible to implement is a duty as much as possible.

Nascent Rule

Confirmation of rule and governance for the imam does not mean stripping him of the status which he has with God and does not make him like other rulers. The imam has a commendable status, a sublime rank and nascent rule to whose control all the particles of this universe are subject. It is one of the essentials of our creed that our imams possess that which no favored king and no dispatched prophet possesses. According to the narrations and the Hadiths we have, the prophet and the imams were, before the creation of this world, lights and God set them around His throne and gave them a status and a place that only God knows. The angel Jibra'il (Gabriel) says in the tales of al-Mi'raj (prophet's midnight journey to the seven heavens): "Had I come a hair's breadth nearer, I would have been burned." The imams are quoted as having said: "We have with God states that no favored king nor a dispatched prophet approaches." Such a place is held by Fatimah al-Zahra', peace be upon her, not because she was a caliph, a ruler or a judge because the place of rule, caliphate or amirate is something else. When we say that Fatimah was not a judge, a ruler or a caliph, then this does not mean that she does not possess that favored status, and it also doesn't mean that she was an ordinary woman, like the women we have. If somebody says that the prophet is above the faithful, then he has given the prophet a place beyond that of being a ruler or a governor of the faithful. We do not object to this and we rather support it, even though this is something that only God knows.

Government Is Means for Achieving Sublime Goals

Running state affairs does not give those in charge of running them a higher place and status because the government is a means for implementing the laws and for establishing the just Islamic system. Government is deprived of all value if it comes to be considered a goal sought for itself. The amir of the faithful ('Ali) once said to Ibn 'Abbas, while the amir was mending the sole of a shoe: What is the worth of this sole? Ibn 'Abbas said: It has no value. The imam said: By God it is worth more to me than being your amir, unless I set matters aright or prevent an injustice. The imam was not running after the governorship nor was he fond of it. He says: "By Him Who split the seed and created the breeze, were it not for the presence of the Omnipresent and of the presence of the proof of the existence of the Victory Giver and for God's demand from the ulema not to condone the injustice of a tyrant and the suffering of the wronged, I would let matters go, would mix up its end with its beginning, and you would find this world of yours less significant to me than a goat's sneeze."

Governing is not an end in itself. It is a means of value as long as its goal is noble. If sought as a goal and if all means are used to attain it, then it degenerates to the level of a crime and its seekers come to be considered criminals. Our imams did not have the opportunity to take charge of affairs even though they waited for this opportunity to the end of their lives. The just jurisprudents must wait for opportunities and must exploit them to form and organize a wise government intended to carry out God's order and to establish a just system, even though this may require strenuous efforts from them. The jurisprudent's taking charge of people's affairs as much as possible represents in itself obedience to God's order and a performance of the duty required by the Shari'a.

A proof that government is a means and not a goal is what the amir of the faithful said in the speech that he made in the Prophet's Mosque after he was given the pledge of allegiance by the people. The amir said: "God, You know that what we have done was not to compete for power nor to seek the ephemeral things of this world but to restore the landmarks of your religion and to achieve reform in your land so that the wronged among your people may gain security and that your obstructed strictures may be carried out."

Qualities of Ruler
Who Achieves These Goals

In this same speech, the amir of the faithful points out the qualities that must be present in the ruler who wants to achieve the sublime goals mentioned by the imam in his speech. The imam says: "God, I am the first to deputize, to hear and to answer, preceded to prayer only by the prophet of God, may God's peace and prayers be upon him. You have learned that the ruler must not be a womanizer, and must not be bloodthirsty, a seeker of gains, of governance, and of leadership of the Moslems. He must not be greedy because he will covet what they possess, must not be ignorant because he will mislead them with his ignorance, must not be rough because he will alienate them with his roughness, must not be fearful because he will favor some over others, must not be a taker of bribes because he will cause rights to be lost and must not obstruct the Sunna because he will cause the nation to perish."

All this revolves, as you can see, around the ruler's knowledge and justice. They are two conditions that must be present in the Moslem ruler. The amir of the faithful says: "And he must not be ignorant because he will mislead them with his ignorance." In these words, the amir of the faithful refers to the first condition. In the rest of his Hadith, he refers to justice, which means that the ruler must follow the example of the amir of the faithful in his rule, his relations and his association with the people. The ruler must also follow the instructions that the amir of the faithful issued to Malik al-Ashtar, the man whom he appointed to rule Egypt. We can consider these instructions addressed to all rulers, governors and jurisprudents in every time and every place.

RULE OF JURISPRUDENT INDICATED BY HADITHS

Successors of Prophet, May God's Peace and Prayers Be Upon Him, Are Just Jurisprudents

Ali, the amir of the faithful, said that the prophet of God said thrice: "God have mercy upon my successors." So he was asked: "O prophet of God, who are your successors?" He said: "Those who come after me, transmit my statements and my laws and teach them to the people after me." *

Shaykh al-Saduq, may God have mercy upon him, mentions this narration in Jami' al-Akhbar, in 'Uyun Akhbar al-Rida and in al-Majalis (all Hadith books) in five different versions, or at least in four versions, because two relaters have a common name. When this narration is mentioned unquoted, it does not include the phrase "and they will teach them to

* Author of Wasa'il al-Shi'a (Shi'ite Means) mentions this Hadith in the Book of the Judiciary, in the eighth chapter concerning the qualities of the modern qadi (judge) and also in detail in Chapter 11. This Hadith is also mentioned in Ma'ani al-Akhbar Wa al-Majalis (Meaning of Messages and of Councils) in two versions and from a number of narrators, some of whom share the same name. It is also mentioned in three different versions in 'Uyun Akhbar al-Rida (Sources of Good News).

the people after me." When quoted from various sources, the narration contains the phrase "and will teach them to the people" in some versions and "will teach them" in other versions.

Our discussions on this Hadith will focus on two assumptions:

1. Let us assume that this narration was relayed by al-ahad (meaning people who misquoted the original statements of the prophet) and that the phrase "and will teach them" was added to the Hadith or assume that the phrase was in fact there but was dropped—and this is a more feasible assumption because we cannot accuse the three relaters of collusion to add this phrase, considering that there was no tie binding them—one of them lived in Balakh, the other in Nisabur and the third in Maru—that they lived very far apart, and that they did not know one another. Therefore, we can say decisively that the phrase "and will teach them" in the version relayed by al-Saduq was dropped by the scribes or that al-Saduq forgot it.

2. Let us assume that there are two versions, one of them without the phrase "and they will teach them" and the other containing this phrase. Let us assume that this phrase is present in the Hadith. The Hadith does still not include decisively those whose sole preoccupation is to relay the Hadith without study and examination and without interpretation, without making conclusions, and without the ability to reach a realistic judgment. We cannot describe such relaters as being qualified for the succession as long as they are mere transmitters or scribes of the Hadith who hear it and relay it to the people. We say this while acknowledging the value of the service that they offer Islam. The mere transmission and relay of the Hadith is not something that qualifies the transmitter or relater to succeed the prophet, because some transmitters and relaters might be the embodiment of the phrase "there may be a transmitter of jurisprudence who is not a jurisprudent." This does not mean that there are no

jurisprudents among the transmitters and relaters, because many are the transmitters who are jurisprudents, such as al-Killini, Shaykh al-Saduq and his father, who were jurisprudents who taught the people. When we differentiate between Shaykh al-Saduq and Shaykh al-Mufid, we do not mean by this distinction that Shaykh al-Saduq was not a jurisprudent or that he was a lesser jurisprudent than Shaykh al-Mufid.

How can we say this when it is said that Shaykh al-Saduq explained the religious fundaments and subsidiaries in one session. The difference between the two is the Shaykh al-Mufid exerts more efforts to make conclusions and examines the narrated versions of the Hadith more carefully and closely.

This Hadith is intended for those who seek to spread the sciences and laws of Islam and to teach them to the people, as the prophet and the imams taught and graduated thousands of ulema. If we say that Islam is the religion of the world, and this is clear and obvious, then the ulema of Islam must spread and disseminate the laws of this religion in the entire world.

Assuming that the phrase "teach them to the people" is not part of the Hadith, let us examine what the prophet's phrase "God have mercy upon my successors who will come after me and relate my statements and my laws" means.

In this respect, the Hadith does not mean the relaters to the exclusion of the jurisprudents because the prophet's law is the law of God and whoever wants to disseminate it must know all the divine laws, must be able to distinguish the correct Hadiths from the false ones, must be familiar with the general and with the particular and with what is absolute and what is restricted and must be able to combine them knowledgeably and rationally. He must also know the versions related under conditions forcing the imams to resort to dissimulation and preventing them from demon strating the real judgments in certain cases. A Hadith transmitter who has not reached the rank of interpretation and who is just entrusted with transmitting the Hadith cannot reach the truth of the law. In the opinion of the prophet, such a transmitter of the Hadith is of no weight. It is well known that the prophet did not want the people to be content with saying "the prophet, may God's peace and prayers be upon him, said . . ." or "the messenger of God is quoted as having said . . ." The prophet did not want the people to be content with this, regardless of the way the Hadith was quoted and related. The quotation "God will make whoever preserves for my nation forty Hadiths a jurisprudent" and other quotations that glorify those who seek to spread the Hadith are not intended to mean the relater who does not understand what he relates and who perhaps is transmitting to someone who understands more than him. These quotations are intended for those who teach people the real laws of Islam. This cannot be done except by a learned jurisprudent who teaches the actual laws and derives them from their sources in accordance with the criteria set for him by Islam and by the imams themselves. These interpreters of religion are the successors to the messenger of God. They spread the Sunna and the sciences of Islam and teach and convey them to the people. This is why they deserve the prophet's invocation in God's mercy for them.

There is no doubt then that the Hadith "god have mercy upon my successors . . ." has nothing to do with those who merely transmit the Hadith without any jurisprudence because the mere scribing of the Hadith does not qualify a person to succeed the prophet. Those meant by the phrase are the jurisprudents of Islam who simplify the teachings and ethics of Islam and who combine justice and true religion with their jurisprudence and knowledge.

A jurisprudent distinguishes those who may be quoted from those who may not be quoted. There are among the relaters of the Hadith those who have falsified Hadiths in the name of the prophet. A relater like Samrah ibn Jandab falsifies Hadiths that undermine the prestige of the amir of the faithful. There are perhaps relaters who do not refrain from transmitting thousands of hadiths praising unjust rulers and their good conduct through the aides of darkness and the ulema of the court in order to glorify the sultans and justify their actions. Such a thing is happening at present, as you can see. I do not know why some people cling to two weak hadiths in contrast to the Koran in which God orders Moses to rise in the face of Pharaoh, who is a king, and in contrast to the many Hadiths that order that the unjust be fought and resisted. The idle ones among the people are the ones who put aside all this to cling to two hadiths that honor kings and justify cooperating with them. Were such people truly religious, they would cite these two Hadiths side by side with the Hadiths that are opposed to the unjust and to their supporters. Such relaters of the Hadith are just because they align themselves with the enemies of God, because they steer away from the correct teachings of the Koran and the Sunna and because their gluttony, and not their knowledge, is what made them do such a thing. The love of glory motivates some people to march with the bandwagon of tyrants.

Therefore, dissemination of Islam's laws and sciences is a task performed by just jurisprudents who can differentiate right from wrong and who are aware of the conditions under which the imams lived and which led to dissimulation to which the imams had to resort to preserve the creed from obliteration and not necessarily to save their lives.

There is no place for doubting that the Hadith indicates that the jurisprudent is the ruler and the successor in all affairs. The succession referred to in the phrase "God have mercy upon my successors" is no different from the succession referred to in the phrase "'Ali is my successor."

The phrase "those who come after me and relay my statements" describes the character of the successor and does not explain the meaning of the succession because at the outset of Islam, succession was a clear concept. It was clear even to the person asking the question who did not ask the prophet about the meaning of the succession but rather asked him: "Who are your successors?"

Nobody considered the position of a caliph in the days of the amir of the faithful and in the day of the imams following him as a position of interpretation solely. Rather, the Moslems interpreted this position as a position of rule and governance and of carrying out God's orders and they cited too many proofs to be mentioned here in support of their interpretation. But why do some of us pause before the meaning of the phrase "God have mercy upon my successors?" Why do these people think that the succession to the prophet's position is confined to a certain person? In view of the fact that the imams were the successors to the prophet, then other ulemas may not rule and manage the affairs of people and let the Moslems remain without a legitimate ruler, let the laws of Islam remain idle and let the borders of the Moslems remain open. This thinking and this postion are far from Islam because it is a devious thinking which Islam disavows.

Muhammad ibn Yahya, citing Ahmad ibn Muhammad who quoted Ibn Mahbub who quoted 'Ali ibn Abi Hamzah, said: "I heard Abu-al-Hasan Musa ibn Ja'far, peace be upon him, say: 'When the faithful dies, the angels, the lands in which he worshipped God and the gates of heaven toward which he rose with his actions weep for him, and he leaves in Islam an irreparable loss because the jurisprudents are the strongholds of Islam as the Medinas's wall is its stronghold." *

* Al-Kafi, Fadl al-'Ilm (Virtues of Knowledge), Loss of Ulema chapter, Third Hadith.

A Look at Text of This Hadith

The same chapter of al-Kafi's book contains another version of this Hadith which says "when the faithful jurisprudent dies . . .", whereas the first part of this version of the Hadith does not contain the word "jurisprudent." But it is indicated by the last part of the previous Hadith which says "because the faithful jurisprudents . . ." that the word "jurisprudent" dropped from the first part of the Hadith, considering that this word is compatible with the prophet's phrase "loss for Islam" and his use of the word "stronghold" and similar words compatible with the status of faithful jurisprudents.

On Meaning of Hadith

His words "because the faithful jurisprudents are the strongholds of Islam . . ." is an assignment to the jurisprudents to preserve Islam with its creeds, laws and systems. This statement was not made by the imam in praise or commendation or as part of the general courtesy acknowledged among us, like when I tell you that you are the authoritative source of Islam and you tell me something similar.

If a jurisprudent isolates himself from the people and their affairs and lives in a corner of his house, if he fails to preserve and disseminate the laws of Islam, to exert efforts to reform the affairs of Moslems, and if he does not care for Moslems, can he be considered a stronghold of Islam or a wall protecting it?

If the government head sends a person to a small subdistrict and orders him to tend and preserve it, does this man's duty permit him to stay in his home and to wreak corruption on that subdistrict or does his job require him to exert all his efforts to tend and preserve what he is entrusted with?

If you say we will keep some of the laws, then I will ask you this question:

Will you carry out the strictures and apply the penal code of Islam?

No!

Then You have created a crack in the edifice of Islam that should have been repaired and mended or should have been prevented from occurring in the first place.

Will you defend the borders and safeguard the security and independence of the lands of Islam?

No, we beseech God to do this!

Here, another side of the edifice has collapsed, in addition to the side that had already collapsed.

Will you collect the dues of the poor that are imposed by God on the money of the rich and give these dues to those who deserve them in implementation of what God has ordered?

No! This is not our concern. God willing, this will be achieved at the hands of others.

What remains of the edifice? The structure is about to be ruined. In this regard, you are like Shah Sultan Husayn and Asfahan.

What stronghold of Islam are you? As soon as one of you is entrusted with preserving something, he declines! Is what is meant by the stronghold of Islam your current situation?

His words that "the jurisprudents are the strongholds of Islam" means that they are entrusted with preserving Islam with all their power. Preserving Islam is one of the most important, absolute and unconditional duties. This is what the religious academies and councils must think of thoroughly so that they may prepare themselves with agencies, resources and conditions under which the laws, creeds and rules are preserved and safeguarded, as the great prophet and the guided imams preserved Islam.

We have been content with discussing a few rules concerning succession and we have discussed numerous aspects and details of this issue. Much of what we have discussed is strange to us. Islam in its entirety has become strange to us and what remains of it is its name. Its penalties have been disregarded and the penalties specified by the Koran are recited as mere phrases. Only the form of Islam remains. We read the Koran for nothing more than to recite it well. As for the corrupt social situation, the spread of corruption throughout the country under the eyes and ears of the governments or with their support for and with their dissemination of fornication and abomination, this is something with which we are not concerned. It is enough for us to understand that there are certain strictures concerning adulterers and adulteresses. As for implementing these strictures and others, this is not our concern!

We ask: Is this how the great prophet was? Was the prophet content with reciting and singing the phrases of the Koran without establishing its structures and implementing its rules? Were the prophet's successors content with relaying the Shari'a rules to the people and then letting people do whatever they wished to do? Did not the prophet and his successors after him implement the strictures on lashing, stoning, jailing and banishing? Study again the chapter concerning strictures, penalties and blood money to find that all this is of the essence of Islam. Islam came to organize society through the just government that it establishes among the people.

We are entrusted with preserving Islam. This is one of the most important duties and is perhaps a no less important duty than praying and fasting. This is the duty for which noble blood was shed. There is no nobler blood than that of al-Husayn which was shed for the sake of Islam. We must understand this and explain it to the people to understand it. You will be the prophet's successors if you teach the people and familiarize them with the truth of Islam. Do not say we will leave this until al-Hijjah (the expected Shiite leader), may peace be upon him, appears. Would you stop praying while waiting for al-Hijjah? Wouldn't you be saying what other people have said, namely: We must wait until sins spread so that al-Hijjah may appear! This means that if abomination does not spread, then al-Hijjah will not appear! Do not be content with sitting here and discussing private matters. Study the various laws deeply. Spread the facts of Islam. Write and publish what you write because this will influence people, God willing. I have tried this myself.

JURISPRUDENTS ARE REPRESENTATIVES OF PROPHETS

'Ali, citing Abih who quoted al-Nawfali who quoted al-Sukuni who quoted Abi 'Abdallah, said: "The messenger of God, may God's prayers and peace be upon him and upon his kinsmen, said: The jurisprudents are the representatives of the prophets, unless they enter the world. He was asked: O messenger of God, what does their entering the world mean? He said: Follow the sultan. If they do so, then beware of them for your religion." *

* Al-Kafi's book Fadl al-'Ilm (Virtues of Knowledge), Chapter 13, Hadith No 5. This Hadith is also included in what al-Niraqi related. Al-Nuri also transmitted the Hadith in Chapter 38 of the book Mustadrak al-Wasa'il, Hadith No 8, citing the book al-Nawadir by al-Rawandi who quotes correctly Imam Musa iban Ja'far and the book Da'a'im al-Islam (Mainstays of Islam), Chapter 11, on the qualities of the judge, and also quoting Hadith No 5 from Imam Ja'far ibn Muhammad. Al-Kafi's book itself contains another

We cannot examine the Hadith in its entirety because this requires a long discussion. We must examine closely the phrase "the jurisprudents are the representatives of the prophets."

We must first know the duties, tasks, power and the works of the prophets and the messengers so that we may then know the assignments entrusted to the jurisprudents trusted by the prophets.

Aims of Messages

By the dictates of reason, the aim behind the dispatch of messengers is not confined to explaining the laws and rules that they receive by revelation. The prophets were not only assigned to carry out these laws among the people with utter sincerity and the prophets were not content to entrust the jurisprudents with explaining the issues that they learned from them. The phrase "the jurisprudents are the representatives of prophets" does not mean that the jurisprudents are entrusted to only relate what the prophets said. The most important thing with which the prophets were entrusted was to establish a just system in society and to implement the laws. All this can be concluded from His words: "We have sent our messengers with the evidence and we have sent down with them the book and the scales so that they may establish justice among people." * The real aim of sending the prophets was to establish justice among people and to organize their lives in accordance with the criteria of the Shari'a. This can be done only by a government that implements the laws. The same way this government is embodied in the person of the prophet or the messenger, it is

---

Hadith to this effect, citing Abi 'Abdallah, peace be upon him, who said: "Sincere and pious ulema are strongholds and prophets are masters."

* Al-Hadid.

also embodied in the imams and in the learned, faithful and just jurisprudents after they become governing people, and establishing right and a just system is required in all cases.

When God says "Know that one-fifth of what you gain is for God, the prophet and for his kinsmen" * and when He says "Take alms from their monies" ** and when He gives other such orders, then this does not mean that the prophet is not only entrusted to convey this to the people but is also ordered to act upon it and implement it. He is ordered to collect these taxes from the people who should pay them so that he may spend them in the interest of the Moslems. He is ordered to spread justice among the people, to establish the strictures, to protect the borders of the Moslems, to guard the country against the enemies and to prevent anybody from exploiting the nation's treasury. The venerable Koran says: "Obey God, obey the prophet and obey those in charge among you . . ." † This means that we must not only believe what they have told us but must also act upon it and obey it because this pleases God. God says in another part of His book: "Take what the prophet has brought you, refrain from what he had ordered you to refrain from and have the fear of God." ‡ Obedience to the prophet is obedience to God because the prophet does not speak out of whims but out of revelation. If the prophet orders that Usamah's campaign be joined, then nobody has the right to refrain or to question his order because such behavior would be disobedience to the messenger when the messenger is given charge of the affairs of Moslems and assigned to run their affairs, to direct and guide them and to appoint for them provincial rulers, governors and judges, and to dismiss them if necessary.

* Al-Anqal, 43.

** Al-Tawbah, 104.

† Al-Nisa', 63.

‡ Al-Hashr, 7.

Jurisprudents Are Representatives of Messengers in Leading Army, Managing Society, Defending Nation, and Settling Disputes Among Peoples

The above-mentioned Hadith in which the jurisprudents are trusted by the messengers makes it a condition that the jurisprudents refrain from entering the world (becoming obedient to sultan) because a jurisprudent whose concern is to amass ephemeral things is not just, is not trusted by the prophet and does not implement his laws. The just jurisprudents are the only ones qualified to implement the laws and rules of Islam, to establish Islam's strictures and to protect the borders of the Moslems. In any case, the prophets have entrusted the jurisprudents with all the powers to which they themselves were authorized and have trusted them with that which they themselves were trusted with. Thus, the jurisprudents are the ones who collect the taxes to spend them for the good of the Moslems and they are the ones who correct whatever corruption there is in the affairs of Moslems. The prophet was trusted with implementing the laws, establishing the system and so are the jurisprudents to whom the rule belongs and on whose shoulders the burdens of implementing the laws, establishing God's stricture, fighting his enemies and eliminating every source of corruption falls.

Law-abiding Government

In view of the fact that the government of Islam is the government of law, only the jurisprudent, and nobody else, should be in charge of the government. He is the one to undertake what the prophet undertook without adding anything to it or striking away from it. He is the one to establish the strictures as the prophets established them, to govern as God has ordered, to collect the excess monies of people as this was done in the days of the prophet and to organize the treasury and be trusted with it. If the jurisprudent violates the dictates of the Shari'a laws, God forbid, then he is dismissed automatically for lacking the element of trustworthiness. The supreme ruler is, in fact, the law, and all must live under its canopy. People are born free and are free in their legal actions. Nobody has a (special) right over anybody and nobody may, when the law is implemented, force anybody to sit anywhere or to go anywhere unjustly. The government of Islam reassures and secures the Moslems and does not take away their reassurance and security like the governments under which the Moslem lives in fear, expecting them to attack his home at any moment and to take away his life, his money and all he possesses, as you can see with your own eyes. Such a thing happened in the days of Mu'awiyah who used to kill people on mere suspicion and accusation, used to jail people for long times, banish them from the country and who used to unjustly drive people out of their homes for no reason other than their saying God is our God. Mu'awiyah's government did not represent the Moslem government or resemble it closely or remotely. If God wills the Moslem government to arise, and this is not beyond God's will, then everybody will be reassured about his life, his money, his kinsmen and his possessions because no ruler is empowered to carry out among the people acts in violation of the stipulations of the orthodox Islamic law. This is what the word "representative" means. It is well-known, as already pointed out, that representation is not confined to honesty in relaying, transmitting or interpreting only but also includes honesty in action, in application and in implementation, even though honesty in transmitting and interpreting is of great importance. The prophet and the amir of the faithful spoke and acted upon their words and God trusted them with His message. God trusted the messengers and the jurisprudents to speak out, to work, to hold prayers, to collect taxes, to order good deeds and prohibit evil deeds and to run the people's affairs justly. Islam considers the law an instrument and a means for achieving justice in society and a means for polishing man morally, ideologically and practically. The task of the prophets was to embody the law, to settle disputes among people, to run their affairs and to lead them toward their happiness in this world and in the hereafter.

We have already mentioned in this discussion that Imam al-Rida said: "Had He not appointed for them a trusted and pacifying imam, the nation would have perished ..." * In this same Hadith, he says: "The jurisprudents are the representatives of the messengers." It is concluded from the two quotations that the jurisprudents are the ones who should lead the march of the people so that Islam may not perish. The obliteration of Islam and the obstruction of its strictures are actually due to the fact that the jurisprudents in the Moslem countries have not been able to rule the people. Experience has confirmed the imam's opinion as stated in the phrase: "Had He not appointed an imam ... the nation would have perished."

Hasn't Islam been obliterated? Isn't Islam obliterated now? Have not the laws of Islam been obstructed in the many countries of Islam? Are Islam's legislations observed and is its system followed? Isn't the situation one of chaos? Is Islam this ink on paper? Do you think that the sole aim of our religion is to have its laws collected in al-Kafi's book and then be shelved away? Will Islam be preserved if we kiss the Koran, put it on our heads and recite its phrases with a beautiful voice day and night?

Islam has reached this tragic end because we have not thought of organizing society and of bringing it happiness through a Moslem government. Unjust and corrupt laws violating the teachings of Islam have been applied to the Moslems—laws that God has given no power. Islam has

* 'Ilal al-Shara'i' (Causes of Laws), 1/172, Hadith No 9.

almost been obliterated and forgotten in the minds of some of the esteemed gentlemen to the degree that some of them have gone as far as interpreting the phrase "the jurisprudents are the representatives of the prophets" to mean honesty in transmitting the issues. These esteemed gentlemen have also gone as far as interpreting the Koran and Hadith phrases which indicate that the jurisprudents should rule the people in the age of absence as phrases which mean that the jurisprudents should only explain the issues and the laws! Is this the trust? Isn't it the duty of the trusted representatives to keep the laws of Islam actually alive and to guard them against negligence and obstruction? Isn't it the duty of a man trusted with a country not to let the aggressors move without being punished? Isn't it his duty to prevent chaos, to fight heresies and falsehoods and to strike those who tamper with the people's lives and properties? Yes, this is what representation requires and what the trust given to the messengers themselves requires.

Who Should Be Trusted with Judiciary Tasks

Muhammad ibn Yahya, citing Muhammad ibn Ahmad, who quoted Ya'qub ibn Yazid, who quoted Yahya ibn Mubarak, who quotes 'Abdallah ibn Jamyilah, who quoted ishaq ibn 'Ammar, who quoted Abi 'Abdallah, peace be upon him, said: "The amir of the faithful, God's prayers be upon him, said to Shurayh: O Shurayh you have taken a position that only a prophet's guardian or a villain takes." *

This Shurayh occupied the post of a judge for nearly fifty years. He flattered, praised and applauded Mu'awiyah and used to praise him with what Mu'awiyah did not deserve.

* Wasa'il al-Shi'ah (Shiite Means), Book Of Space, Chapter 3, Hadith 2, Man La Yahduruhu al-Faqih (He Who Is Not Visited by Jurisprudent), Part 3, page 4, Relayed in Detail.

This position that he took was tantamount to destroying what the government of the amir of the faithful had built. But 'Ali (the amir of the faithful) could not dismiss Shurayh because those who came before him had appointed him and, therefore, the amir of the faithful was not empowered to dismiss him. However, 'Ali did watch him and did prevent him from committing what was in violation of the teachings of the Shari'a.

Judiciary Matters Are Concerns of Just Jurisprudents

Even though there has been disagreement on the issue of rule and even though some ulemas, such as al-Niraqi and al-Na'ini, may they rest in peace, expressed the belief that the jurisprudent has the same tasks as those of the imam in the spheres of government, administration and policy while others said that the rule of the jurisprudent is not as comprehensive as that of the imam—even though there has been disagreement on this, I do not find that there has been any disagreement on the fact that the position of a judge is exclusively for the just jurisprudent, considering that the quotation mentions the "prophet, villain and guardian." It is well known that the jurisprudents are not prophets and there is no doubt that they are not villains. By necessity, the description "guardian" applies to them. Because the word "guardian" is used predominantly by the amir of the faithful, the first guardian, we find that some people do not accept this quotation as a proof of our issue. We have already said that nobody should imagine that the postion of rule elevated the status of the imams because governing the people and running their affairs was nothing more than carrying out a duty, setting matters aright, reforming society and spreading justice among people. The imams had high positions and ranks that only God knew. Their appointment or non-appointment to the caliphate neither elevated nor lowered their ranks because this position of rule is not what raises the status of a man or makes him important. Whoever is a pious jurisprudent is qualified to occupy this position as a part of his duties in life.

In any case, we understand from the Hadith that the jurisprudents are the prophet's guardians after and in the absence of the imams and that they were entrusted to carry out whatever the imams were entrusted to do.

There is another Hadith that supports our issue and which is perhaps better supported and more indicative. This Hadith was transmitted by al-Killini poorly. Howerver, al-Saduq transmitted it, quoting Sulayman ibn Khalid, who is correct and authoritative.

"Abu 'Abdallah, citing several of our colleagues who quoted Suhayl ibn Ziyah, who quoted Muhammad ibn 'Isa, who quoted Abu 'Abdallah al-Mu'min, who quoted Sulayman ibn Khalid, said: Beware the government because government belongs to an imam who is knowledgeable in Islam and just among Moslems, to a prophet (or like a prophet) or to a prophet's trustee." This quotation was also transmitted by al-Saduq, quoting Sulayman ibn Khalid.*

You can see that whoever governs or dispenses justice among the people must be an imam knowledgeable in the laws and the rules and must be just. These qualities are available only in a prophet or a prophet's trustee. I have already demonstrated that it is axiomatic that the position of the judiciary can only be held by the just jurisprudent. A jurisprudent means a person knowledgeable in the Islamic creeds, laws, rules and ethics, i.e., he is a person who is familiar with all that the prophet brought. The imam confined the judiciary to a prophet or a prophet's trustee.

* Al-Wasa'il, Book of Judiciary, Book 3, Hadith 3, 18/7, Modern Edition.

Considering that the jurisprudent is not a prophet, then he is a prophet's trustee. In the age of the absence, the jurisprudent, and nobody else, is the imam and leader of the Moslems and the person dispensing justice among them justly.

Who Is Authority on Events of Life

The third narration is quoted from al-Qa'im al-Mahdi, the 12th imam, and we will present this narration, explaining the way to benefit from it:

The book Ikmal al-Din Wa Itmam al-Ni'mah (Perfection of Religion and Completion of Blessing), cites Muhammad ibn Muhammad ibn 'Isam, who quoted Muhammad ibn Ya'qub, who cites Ishaq ibn Ya'qub as having said: "I asked Muhammad ibn 'Uthman al-'Umari to dispatch for me a message in which I had asked about issues that posed a problem for me. The answer came signed by our ruler, may peace be upon him: 'As to what you have asked about, may God guide and strengthen you . . .'" This continues until the message reaches the point where the ruler says: "As for the events that have taken place, refer to the transmitters of our statements because they are my authority to you and I am God's authority. As for Muhammad ibn 'Uthman al-'Umari, may God be pleased with him and with his father before him, he has my confidence and his book is mine." *

Naturally, what is meant by the intended events is not the canonical laws and issues. The inquirer knew his authority on these issues and laws. People referred to the jurisprudents when they had a problem with any of the canonical laws and rules. This used to happen even in the days of the imams

* Al-Wasa'il, 18/101, Book of the Judiciary, Chapter 11, Hadith 9, Related by Shaykh al-Tusi in the book al-Ghaybah (Absence) and al-Tubrusi Related It in the book al-Ihtijaj (Protest).

themselves because people were far from the imams and lived in provinces other than that in which the imam lived. The inquirer, who lived at the outset of the age of the absence of the imam and who was in contact with his deputies and who was corresponding with the imam and asking for his opinion, was not asking for the authority on interpretation because he knew this well. He was asking about the authority on the contemporary social problems and on the developments in the people's life. Because it was impossible to refer to the imam due to the latter's absence, the inquirer wanted to know the authority on the changes in life, on society's developments and on transient events and did not know what to do. His question was a general question that was not addressed to a certain authority and the answer was also general and befitting the question. The answer was, as you know: Refer to the transmitters of our statements because they are my authority to you and I am God's authority.

What does "God's authority" mean? What do you understand from it? Does it mean [words illegible]. Does "God's authority" mean that if the ruler, peace be upon him, transmits information about the prophet, then we must accept this information as we accept Zarrarah's information? Does "God's authority" lie in explaining issues and laws only? When the prophet said "I have appointed 'Ali, peace be upon him, as your authority," does this mean: I will go and leave behind 'Ali with you to explain and clarify issues and laws to you? What does it mean?

God's authority means that the imam is the reference to the people on all issues and that God has appointed him and entrusted him to take every action capable of doing the people good and making them happy. The same applies to the jurisprudents. They are the nation's reference and leaders. God's authority is the man appointed by God in charge of the affairs of the Moslems. His actions and his statements are a writ to the Moslems that must be implemented and that must not be allowed to be disregarded in establishing the strictures, collecting the one-fifth, alms, the land and the gains taxes and in spending these taxes. This means that if you refer to the tyrant rulers in the presence of the authority, then you will be held accountable and will be punished for your action on the day of resurrection. God, may He be praised, gives the authority to the amir of the faithful to pursue those who rebelled against Him and disobeyed His order. God also objects to Mu'awiyah and the Ommiad and Abbaside rulers, their aides and their supporters for usurping what was not their right and for holding a position to which they were not qualified.

God brings to account unjust rulers and every government deviating from the teachings of Islam. He makes them account for what they gained, for how they spent the monies of the Moslems, for the monies they wasted on coronation ceremonies and on the 25th centennial anniversary of the rule of sultans in Iran. What will they say when they are brought to account? Perhaps he [sic] will apologize and say: Our special circumstances made this inevitable and called for building the biggest palaces and for excessive and unchecked extravagance in coronation anniversaries and similar occasions for the sake of fame and reputation in the world! He will be asked: Was not 'Ali a good example for you? Was he not a ruler of the Moslems and the amir of a vast nation? Have you done for the people more than the amir of the faithful did for them? Did you want to elevate Islam to a status to which 'Ali had not elevated it? Which of the two states is bigger: yours or his? Your state was nothing more than a single province in his state, which included Egypt, Iraq, Hejaz and Yemen. Despite all this, don't you know that his bureau was in the mosque and that his judiciary platform was in one of the mosque's corners? Didn't you know that he gathered his armies and troops in the mosque to start their march and their movement from that mosque? Didn't you realize that they marched to war confident of themselves and with prayers filling their hearts? Didn't you know how they marched and advanced and how God gave them victories?

Jurisprudents are nowadays the authority to the people as was the prophet their authority. Whatever was trusted to the prophet has been trusted by the imams to the jurisprudents after them. The jurisprudents are the authority on all matters, issues and problems. They have been trusted with governing, ruling and running the affairs of people and with collecting taxes and spending. God will bring to account and punish whoever disobeys them.

This narration that we have cited has a clear significance. If it does not reach the degree of a proof of our opinion, then at least it supports and backs up what we believe.

Phrases from Venerable Koran

There is another narration that supports our topic of discussion, even proves it. This is 'Umar ibn Hanzalah's (Concurrence), which contains a phrase from the Koran. Let us now review some phrases of the Koran and study them somewhat so that we may proceed to this narration and others.

God save me from the evil Satan.

"God orders you to give the trusts to their owners. If you rule among people, then rule justly. God has a (paradise) which He preaches to you and God is omniscient. O you faithful, obey God, obey the prophet and obey those in charge among you. Should you quarrel over something, refer to God and the prophet if you believe in God and the hereafter. This is better for you." *

Some people believe that what is meant by the trust is that money which people deposit with an individual as a trust and the Shari'a laws with which God has trusted the people and whose observance and application is considered as returning

* Al-Nisa' (The Women), 58 & 59.

64

the trust to its owners. The first is a people's trust and the second God's trust. Others interpret the trust as the imamate. This is contained in the meanings of some Hadiths which show that what is meant by this phrase is we, the imams. God ordered the prophet to return the trust—meaning the imamate—to its people, meaning the amir of the faithful who should give it to those after him and so on.

The phrase also says: "If you rule among people, then rule justly." This is addressed to those who hold in their hands the reins of affairs. This address is not intended to the judges alone, even though they issue the rulings because they are a part of the government controlling people's affairs. The judges are not the entire government. It is well known that modern states have three authorities of which the government and the state agencies are formed, namely: the judiciary authority, the legislative authority and the executive authority. God's words "if you rule . . ." are addressed generally to all the individuals of whom these government authorities consist. A just government is one of the components of the trust which must be delivered to its owners and the owners must take the best care of this government. This government must work in accordance with the laws and with the noble Shari'a. A judge in this government must rule justly and fairly, not tyranically and unjustly, and he must derive his rulings from the straight religion. This government's legislative authority revolves in the sphere of the Shari'a teachings and of the general and comprehensive Islamic rules and laws and never exceeds them or violates them. The executive authorities must operate as religion wants them to operate so that they may bring the people happiness and drive away the ghost of poverty, starvation and backwardness from them. These authorities must also establish the strictures, safeguard security and order—all with moderation and balance and without exaggeration or negligence.

After cutting off a thief's hand, the amir of the faithful, may peace be upon him, used to show the thief compassion, treat him kindly, dress his hand and immerse it in oil. A thief thus came to have the greatest love for him. When the amir heard that Mu'awiyah's army raided al-Anbar and that his men seized Christian and Jewish women and took away their earrings and their bracelets, he felt profound grief and sadness and said: "Should a man die of sadness after this, he would not be blamed and would be a worthy man to me." With these strong emotions, the amir used to carry his sword when necessary to cut off the heads of those wreaking havoc on earth. This is justice.

God's messenger is a just ruler. If he orders that a position be occupied or that a corrupting group of people be wiped out, he rules justly because if he fails to do so, he would be violating justice, and because his rule is always in harmony with the requirements of the interests of Moslems, rather than with the requirements of human life in its entirety.

The supreme ruler must consider the public interests. He must not pay attention to emotions and must not fear anybody's censure in serving God. This is why we find that many of the selfish private interests were wiped out due to concern for the public interest. We also find that Islam fought various groups of people for the harm they caused. The prophet, may God's peace and prayers be upon him, annihilated the Bani Qurayzah Jews to the last man because of the harm he realized they were causing the Moslem society, his government and all the people. The ruler's courage and his reputation in God's eyes lie in his implementation of God's orders and in establishing His strictures without being subject to emotions or to whims and also lie in his compassion, kindness, sympathy and concern for people. These two qualities make the ruler a refuge to which the people resort. As for the fear and anxiety that we witness these days, they are the result of the illegitimacy of the actual governments and because government these days gives the idea of domination, selfishness and tyranny. But in a government like the imam's or in any true Moslem government, there is no fear and no grief among the people and a man is fully secure, unless he betrays, behaves unjustly or violates God's strictures.

The Hadith says that His words, may He be praised, "give the trusts to their owners" pertain to the imams, that His words "if you rule among the people ..." pertain to the amirs and that His words "obey God" are a general address to all the Moslems ordering them to obey those in charge, meaning the imams, to learn from them and to obey their orders.

You have already learned that what is meant by obedience to God is to follow His orders in all the laws of the Shari'a, both the laws pertaining to worship and to other affairs; that obedience to the prophet means following all his orders, including those pertaining to organizing and coordinating society and those pertaining to preparing the material and moral force to defend it, and that this obedience is also obedience to God. Your obedience to the messenger means obeying the instruction he issues to you. If he instructs you to join Usamah's army, to take position on the borders, to pay or to collect taxes and to associate with people kindly, then you must not disobey. God ordered us to take what the prophet has allowed us and to refrain from what he has ordered us not to do. God has also ordered us to take orders from the people in charge, namely the imams, peace be upon them, keeping in mind that obeying the messenger and obeying those in charge is obedience to God because our obeying them reflects our obedience to God's order that we obey them.

The last part of the phrase says: "Should you quarrel over something, refer to God and the prophet if you believe in God and the hereafter. This is better for you." Disputes among people may be over legal issues on which the judge must decide in accordance with evidence and faith. The dispute may not be over a legal matter. It may be a penal issue—an issue of an injustice, attack, murder, theft or something else. In such cases, the matter must be referred to the authorities concerned so that they may act upon these penal or dual—meaning both legal and penal—cases and must issue their sentences in accordance with what the Shari'a orders.

The Koran instructs us to refer all these cases, be they legal or penal, to the messenger in his capacity as the head of the state. He, in turn, is ordered to establish what is right and what is false. After the messenger come the imams and after them come the just jurisprudents.

God, may He be praised, then says: "Have you not seen those who claim that they believe in what has been revealed to you and what was revealed before you wishing to seek the ruling of the false god which they have been ordered to disavow."* What is meant by the false god is every judiciary or governmental authority that bases its rulings on that which God has given no power and every authority that acts unjustly, sinfully and aggressively. God has ordered us to disavow such a thing and to rebel against every unjust government, even if this causes us hardships and difficulties.

'Umar ibn Hanzalah's (Concurrence)

Now, let us examine this (concurrence) and see what is meant by it.

Muhammad ibn Ya'qub, citing Muhammad ibn Yahya who quoted Muhammad ibn al-Husayn, who quoted Muhammad ibn 'Isa who quoted Safwan ibn Yahya who quoted Dawud ibn al-Husayn, said: "I asked Abu 'Abdallah, peace be upon him, about two of our friends who had quarreled over a debt or an inheritance and who went to the sultan and to the courts to settle their dispute and whether this was permissible. He said: Whoever has sought the arbitration of

* Al-Nisa' (The Women), 63.

the sultan and of the courts has sought the arbitration of the false god. Whoever is given the favorable sentence will take whatever he takes unjustly, even if what he takes is his proven right, because he will have taken it by the rule of the false god and the rule of that which God has ordered us to disavow. God has said: 'They wish to seek the rule of the false god when they have been ordered to disavow it.' I said: What should they do? He said: Let them look among you for someone who has been transmitted our Hadith, who has examined our permissibles and our prohibitions and who has learned our rules and let them accept him as an arbitrator because I have made such a man your ruler . . ."*

Ban on Seeking Arbitration of Unjust Rulers

In the first part of his answer to the inquirer's question, the imam prohibited altogether referring to the unjust rulers in legal or penal cases. This means that whoever refers to them is seeking the judgment of the false god which God has ordered us to disavow. The Shari'a orders us not to follow what the unjust rulers order: "He takes it unjustly, even if it is his proven right." A Moslem is prohibited from seeking the arbitration of false gods on a debt that somebody owes him and if he collects his debt in accordance with their rule and sentence, then he is not permitted to dispose of what he is given. Some jurisprudents have said that even in in-kind cases, it is not permitted to take the repossessed article, such as a cloak, and to dispose of it, if it is regained in accordance with the order and rule of false gods.

This (concurrence) is a political ruling that urges the Moslems to stop referring to the tyrannical authorities and their judiciary agencies so that they may go out of business when

* Al-Wasa'il, Chapters on Qualities of Ruler, Chapter 11, Hadith 1, Volume 18, page 98.

the people desert them and so that the door may be opened for the imams and for those appointed by the imams to dispense justice among the people. The true purpose of this narration is that the tyrannical rulers must not be a reference on people's affairs because God has prohibited referring to them and has ordered that they be abandoned and isolated and that they and their rule be disavowed because of their tyranny, injustice and deviation from the straight path.

Moslem Ulema Are Authorities on All Matters

According to what the imam has been quoted to say, the authority is the person who relates their ¿imams'¡ Hadiths, knows their permissibles and their prohibitions and examines their rulings thoroughly in accordance with the interpretation criteria at his disposal. In his answer to the question cited in the narration, the imam left nothing ambiguous or unclear. He required as a condition in the authority, in addition to relating the Hadith, that he know what is permissible and what is taboo and that he be discerning and perceptive because a Hadith relater who is not discerning and perceptive is not an authority.

Ulema Appointed to Rule

Abu 'Abdallah says: "I have appointed him your ruler." The people must accept him as a ruler to whom they refer in their issues and their disputes. Settling disputes is in the power of those whom the imam has appointed, and nobody else. This Shari'a rule applies to all Moslems and is not confined to 'Umar ibn Hanzalah's problem for which the imam gave the answer. As the amir appointed the provincial rulers and ordered people to refer to them and to obey them, so did the faithful imam in his capacity as a ruler and a governor of the

Moslems and over the ulema and the jurisprudents. The imam appointed rulers and judges during his life and till after his death. This is what he reflected by saying: "I have appointed him your ruler." Rule here is not confined to judiciary matters but also includes others. It is concluded from this phrase, the preceding phrases and the narration that the imam's answer is not concerned with the appointment of judges solely and that it is more comprehensive. The narration is undoubtedly clear in its meaning and significance. There is no doubt that the imam appointed the jurisprudents to the government and the judiciary and ordered all the Moslems to take this into consideration.

To further explain and clarify the issue, we will now move to Abu Khadijah's narration:

Muhammad ibn Hasan, citing Muhammad ibn 'Ali ibn Mahjub who quoted Ahmad ibn Muhammad who quoted Husayn ibn Sa'id who quoted Abu al-Jahm who quoted Abu Khadijah, said: "Abu 'Abdallah sent me to some of our friends saying: Tell them: If a dispute or a disagreement erupts between you, beware of going to those profligates for a ruling. Select from among you a person who knows our permissibles and our prohibitions, I will make him your judge. I warn you not to take your disputes to the unjust sultan."*

What is meant by the profligates are the judges appointed by the rulers at that time. In a previous narration, he prohibited referring to the unjust rulers and judges whereas in this narration he appoints the judge who should be consulted. In Hanzalah's concurrence, he appointed the executing ruler and the judge. (It is evident from the last part of the narration that the sultans were the authority for settling some disputes without such disputes being reviewed by the judges.)

* Al-Wasa'il, 18/100, Hadith 6.

71

Were Ulema Dismissed from Position of Rule?

You may wonder whether the rulers and the judges whom the imam appointed during his life, according to the hadiths and especially according to 'Umar ibn Hanzalah's narration, and whom he entrusted with governmental and judiciary affairs were dismissed from their positions after his death or not.

We know that the orders of the imams are different from the orders of others. In our creed, all the orders issued by the imams during their life ocntinue to be in force after their death and must be obeyed even after their death. So what is the opinion in regard to those appointed by the imam specifically or generally as rulers or judges?

In states, whether monarchic, republican or any other type, if the president or the king dies or if a coup d'etat occurs, then all this does not affect the military and administrative ranks automatically, even though the new regime may change and replace those occupying such positions. However, the ranks are not abolished automatically. We find that some matters vanish automatically such as when, for example, a jurisprudent deputizes a person in a certain country or grants a license or (guardianship) to a certain person. Such a deputization or license vanishes with the death of the jurisprudent. But if the jurisprudent appoints a trustee over a minor or appoints somebody in charge of waqf (religious property), then such appointment is not affected by the death of the jurisprudent and continues after his death. Of what type is the appointment of jurisprudents for rule and judgment among the people?

Position of Ulema Is Always Preserved

We believe that the position that the imams granted the jurisprudents is still preserved for the jurisprudents. We cannot imagine the imams to be forgetful or negligent and we believe that they were familiar with all that was in the interest of the moslems. The imams were aware that this position of the jurisprudents would not vanish after their death. If the imam knew that the appointment was meant to be for his lifetime, then he should have drawn the attention of the people to this fact and would have explained to them that the position of the jurisprudents is dependent on the life of the imams and that the jurisprudents are to be dismissed after the death of the imams.

Therefore, in accordance with this narration, the ulema were appointed by the imam for government and for judgment among the people and their position is still preserved for them. We do not find it likely that the imam who came after Imam al-Sadiq dismissed the jurisprudents from this position because this is a weak and improbable likelihood. The imam, peace be upon him, prohibits referring to the unjust rulers and judges and considers referring to them tantamount to referring to the false god. He clings to the Koran phrase in which God orders that the false god be disavowed. If the succeeding imam dismissed those jurisprudents from their position and did not appoint others, then to whom should the Moslems refer in their disputes and conflicts?

We are confident that Imam Musa ibn Ja'far could not have revoked what Imam al-Sadiq had ordered in this regard and in other spheres. He could not have prohibited referring to the just jurisprudents, could not have ordered that the rule of the false god be consulted or could have accepted the loss of rights, properties or lives. The imam does not revoke the general bases which his predecessor has explained and advocated. However, an imam can change rulers or judges in his lifetime if the public interest requires such a change. This is not considered a revocation of what the predecessor adopts.

Here is another narration in support of this, even though the previous ones have been very clear and evident. All these narrations corroborate what we have concluded.

Qaddah's Version (of Narration)

'Ali ibn Ibrahim, citing his father who quoted Hammad ibn 'Isa who quoted al-Qaddah ('Abdallah ibn Maysun) who quoted Abu 'Abdallah, said: "God's messenger, may God's peace and prayers be upon him, said: Whoever follows a path seeking knowledge, then God leads him on a path to paradise. The angels lower their wings over the seeker of knowledge for joy with him. Those in heaven, those on earth and even the whale in the sea is asked for forgiveness for the seeker of knowledge. The superiority of the 'alim (man of knowledge) over the worshipper is like that of the moon over the other stars in a night when the moon is full. Ulema (plural of 'alim) are the heirs to the prophets. The prophets did not leave a single dinar or dirham for inheritence but left knowledge as their inheritance and whoever has taken from this knowledge has acquired a large share."*

The Hadith is correct. Even 'Ali ibn Ibrahim (Ibrahim ibn Hashim), who is one of the main authorities, has transmitted this Hadith. This same Hadith has been transmitted with a slight difference in the text, through another weak channel, meaning a channel in which some of the people quoted are weak, even though the rest of the Hadith is correct. This Hadith ultimately ends with Abu al-Bakhtari who is weak (unreliable source). Because of him, the Hadith weakens.

* Al-Kafi, Part 1. Chapter on Reward of Scholar and of Learner.

Abu al-Bakhtari's Version

Muhammad ibn Yahya, citing Ahmad ibn Muhammad ibn 'Isa who quoted Muhammad ibn Khalid who quoted Abu al-Bakhtari who quoted Abu 'Abdallah, said: "The ulema are the heirs to the prophets, even though the prophets did not leave a single dirham or dinar for inheritance. However, they left their Hadith. Whoever learns a part of their Hadith has taken a large share. Beware, whom you take your knowledge from because there are among us, the kinsmen of the prophet, just successors who prevent the distortion of the fanatics, the falsification of the liars and the interpretation of the ignorant."

Our goal in citing this version of the Hadith to which al-Niraqi adhered is to explain the meaning of the phrase "the heirs to the prophets" mentioned in this Hadith.

1. What is meant by the ulema? Some find it likely that what is meant are the imams. The truth is that what is meant is the Moslem ulema, by evidence of the fact that the qualities of the imams make it unimaginable that this phrase could mean them or that this Hadith could be describing them under any circumstances. In Abu al-Bakhtari's version, after the phrase "the ulema are the heirs to the prophets," the Hadith says: "Beware whom you take your knowledge from." It is unimaginable that this could be addressed to the imams, peace be upon them, because whoever is aware of their status with God's messenger states decisively that what is meant by the ulema in both versions is not the imams but the ulema. This is not an excessive or surprising tribute to the ulema, considering what had been said in their praise and veneration earlier: "The ulema of my nation are like the other prophets before me" and "the ulema of my nation are like the prophets of the sons of Israel." In any case, what is meant by the ulema are the ulema of the Moslem nation.

2. Somebody may protest, saying: The governance of the jurisprudent cannot be concluded from the phrase "the ulema are the heirs to the prophets" because this inheritance may refer to the knowledge of rules and laws that the prophets were given. On this basis, the inheritance does not include governance over the people's affairs because the governance, imamship and leadership of the people can only be confirmed on another basis. Moreover, the Hadith is not as explicit as the phrase "the ulema have the status of Moses and Jesus" to conclude from it the governance of the jurisprudents.

In reply to this objection, I say: The criterion in understanding the Hadiths is to take the apparent meaning of their words. This, and not scientific analyses and laboratory tests, is the acknowledged tradition and understanding. If a jurisprudent were to use scientific analyses and philosophical precision, he may miss many things. If we refer to tradition in understanding the phrase "the ulema are the heirs to the prophets" and ask this tradition if the phrase means that the prophets" and ask this tradition if the phrase means that the jurisprudent has the status of Moses and Jesus, it would say: Yes. Considering that Moses and Jesus are prophets, then the ulema have the status of prophets. If we ask tradition if the jurisprudent is the heir to God's messenger, it would say yes for the same aforementioned reasons. We do not take prophecy to mean the mere receiving of revelation or knowledge of the rules and the laws. If this is likely in the singular case, it is unlikely in the word "prophets" in its plural form. The use of the word prophets in the plural form is intended for all the prophets and not only to the prophets who received nothing but revelation. It includes the prophets who are also rulers. Depriving the prophets of every quality and every significance other than that of knowledge and revelation and reducing the status of the ulema to that of dealing with the rules and the laws constitutes a faulty understanding that is in violation of the tradition of the wisemen.

3. Even if we liken the ulema to the prophets, then we must give the ulema the qualities of that whom we liken them to.

For example, if we say: So and so has the status of a just man and a just man must be honored, then we understand that so and so must be honored. We can conclude from the words of God, may He be praised, "the prophet (is more entitled to rule the Moslems than they are to rule themselves)"* that the position of governance is also confirmed for the ulema by evidence of the fact that the reference pertains, at least, to rule and governance, as stated by the Hadith of Imam al-Baqir in Majma' al-Bahrayn (Confluence of the Two Seas) in comment on this phrase. The imam says: "The phrase was revealed in connection with governance, meaning the amirate."** The prophet is, thus, the ruler of the faithful and their amir. All this is also confirmed for the ulema. The phrase mentions the prophet as a prophet without adding any other consideration.

4. Perhaps there are those who may say that the prophet's inheritance is confined to the Hadiths that he left, that whoever has learned some of these Hadiths has inherited the prophet and that this does not prove the jurisprudent's inheritance of the position of public rule and governance. The Hadith does not go beyond leaving the inheritance of knowledge. Abu al-Bakhtari's version says: "They left their Hadiths for inheritance."

This objection is incorrect because it is established on the basis of the impossibility of inheriting the rule and the amirate. We, as you know, proceed in our understanding on the basis of tradition. If we ask all rational people in the world about the heir to a certain throne, would they say it is impossible to inherit the throne? Or will they point out to us the heir to the throne and the crown? Rule, like other things, may be transferred to others in the view of the rational people. If we examine His words, may He be praised, "the prophet is more entitled to rule the Moslems than they are

* Al-Ahzab (The Parties), 6.

** Majma' al-Bahrayn, 457, Modern Edition.

entitled to rule themselves" and if we reflect upon the prophet's words "the ulema are the heirs to the prophets" we realize that governance is a subjective matter that can be transmitted and that this is not impossible in tradition. Even if we assume that the phrase "the ulema are the heirs to the prophets" is meant for the imams, as some narrations say, we still have no doubt that what is meant by this inheritance is the imams' inheritance of prophets in all matters, not only in laws and knowledge.

Consequently, if we take the phrase "the ulema are the heirs to the prophets" and disregard the first and last parts of the Hadith, we become confident that all the messenger's affairs can be transmitted and inherited, including rule over the people and taking charge of their affairs, and that all this was confirmed for the imams after the prophet and for the juris-prudents after the imams, excluding from this that which the prophet reserved for himself, with external evidence. We exclude what evidence has been excluded so that what has not been excluded may remain as it is and may be an authority for general application.

What strengthens the suspicion that the phrase "the ulema are the heirs to the prophet" is meant only for inheritance of the Hadith and nothing else is the fact that the phrase comes within other phrases which can act as proof of this suspicion. Moreover, Qaddah's version says that "the prophets did not leave a single dinar or dirham for inheritance but left knowl-edge" and al-Bakhtari's version "they did not leave a single dirham or dinar for inheritance. However, they left their Hadith" are suitable proofs that the inheritance is confined to the Hadith and that the prophets left no other inheritance, especially with the use of the word "however" in the latter version. This word (in Arabic) is used for restriction.

This suspicion is weak because of what the prophet left for inheritance is the Hadith and nothing else, then this is in conflict with the essence of the creed because the prophet who was in charge of all the affairs of people appointed the amir of the faithful as ruler of the people after him. The imamate and governance continued to be transmitted from imam to imam until it ended with the existing imam.

Added to this is the fact that it has not been proven that the word "however" was used for restriction. The word "however" does not exist in Qaddah's version even though it is included in Abu al-Bakhtari's version. It has already been pointed out that this version is weak insofar as quotation is concerned.

Let us examine the correct version to find out if it contains proof that the inheritance is restricted to the Hadith or not.

"Whoever follows a path seeking knowledge, God will lead on a path to paradise." This phrase contains praise for the ulema. In regard to the definition of an 'alim (religious scholar or knowledgeable man), refer to al-Kafi who details the 'alim's qualities and duties to learn that this description is not given to anybody who acquires a small degree of knowledge and that there are conditions and restrictions that make attaining this description difficult.

"The angels lower their wings over the seeker of knowledge for joy with him." This is respect, esteem and veneration.

"The forgiveness of those in heaven, those on earth and even of the whale in the sea is asked for the seeker of knowledge ..." This sentence requires a detailed explanation which is outside the framework of our discussion.

"The superiority of the 'alim over the worshipper is like the superiority of the moon over the other stars on a night when the moon is full." The meaning of this phrase is clear.

"The ulema are the heirs to the prophets ..." This is one of the virtues and tributes of the ulema, in addition to their other qualities which have been mentioned in this discussion. The ulema's inheritance of the prophets is a virtue if the ulema take the place of the prophets in ruling the people and running all their affairs.

As for the latter part of the Hadith which says "the prophets did not leave a single dinar or dirham for inheritance . . ," this does not mean that they only left knowledge, the Shari'a and the laws for an inheritance. This phrase means that despite the control they had over people's affairs and despite the power and the authority in their hands, the prophets did not have the greed to be preoccupied with the good things of life, to acquire ephemeral things and to pay attention to the paraphernalia of life. This simple way of life which the prophets lived despite the power they had in their hands is totally different from the luxury and the extravagance lived by the present-day sultans and members of governments which have become a means for excessive and illicit aggrandization.

The prophet's life was one of utter simplicity. He himself did not possess any money and he left behind a knowledge that is nobler than money and whose source is the direct divine revelation. Knowledge and the Hadith are mentioned in these quotations in contrast to money and ephemeral things.

Other Proofs

If we assume that the previously cited quotations indicate the inheritance of only the knowledge, the laws and the rules and that the prophet left nothing else to be inherited, even though the prophet says " 'Ali is my heir," and if we assume that all this does not indicate 'Ali's succession to the rule and 'Ali's governance, then we are compelled to refer to this regard to other sources that indicate the succession of 'Ali ibn 'Abi Talib and the governance of the jurisprudents.

Proofs from al-Ridawi (Reference to the Imam Rida) Jurisprudence

In al-Niraqi's 'Awa'id (Benefits), page 186, Hadith No 7 on al-Ridawi jurisprudence, we find the following quotation: "The jurisprudent's status in these days is like that of the prophets among the sons of Israel."

Naturally, we do not consider all that has been mentioned in al-Ridawi jurisprudence correct. But we will take this Hadith in support of the subject of our discussion.

What is meant by the prophets of the sons of Israel are the jurisprudents living in the time of Moses. Perhaps they were called prophets (for certain reasons). They followed Moses and adopted his ways in their actions and behavior. Whenever Moses sent them somewhere, he put them in charge of the affairs of people in that place. We do not possess accurate and detailed knowledge about their conditions but we know that Moses was one of the prophets of the sons of Israel. Whatever the messenger of Islam was entrusted with, Moses had been entrusted with the same before him, despite the difference in rank and honor. We generally understand from the word "status" which is mentioned in the quotation that the rule and government affairs with which Moses was charged are also confirmed for the ulema.

Another Proof

In Jami' al-Akhbar (Encyclopedia of Information), the prophet is cited as having said: "On the day of resurrection, I will boast of the ulema of my nation and the ulema of my nation are like the other prophets before me." *

* 'Awa'id al-Niraqi, quoting Jami' al-Akbar, page 186, Hadith 6.

Mustadrak al-Wasa'il (The Rectified Means) cites al-Gharar as having said "the ulema are the rulers of the people." This quotation has also been cited as "the ulema are the sages among the people." I do not think the second version is correct because al-Gharar has been quoted as saying "rulers of the people." There are other proofs of the kind.

Tuhaf al-'Uqul Narrations

Tuhaf al-'Uqul (The Gems of the Mind) contains a lengthy narration under the title of: "The Course of Affairs and of Laws on the Hands of the Ulema." The first part of the narration quotes Imam al-Husayn, may peace be upon him, who cites his father, the amir of the faithful, on what he said in connection with encouraging good deeds and prohibiting evil deeds. The second part is a speech addressed by al-Husayn, the master of the martyrs, may peace be upon him, to the people in Muna on the matter of the jurisprudent's governance and his duties to fight the unjust and their states, to destroy such states and to replace them by the legitimate Islamic government. In his speech, al-Husayn made known his reasons for declaring the jihad (holy war) against the tyrannical Ommaiad State. Two things are concluded from this narration: The first is the jurisprudent's governance and the second is the need for the jurisprudent to expose the unjust rulers, to shake their thrones, to awaken and enlighten the people and then to lead them to destroy the tyrannical entity and to replace it by a legitimate Islamic governmental entity. The means to this jihad are ordering good deeds and prohibiting bad deeds. Here is the text (of al-Husayn's speech):

"Learn, o people, from that with which God advised His holymen when He scorned al-Rabbaniyun and al-Ahbar [Christian and Jewish clergymen] with the words: 'Al-Rabbaniyun and al-Ahbar have not ordered then [the rulers] to refrain from speaking evil and from unjust profit. What

82

an evil have they committed.' * God has also said: 'God has execrated the renegades among the sons of Israel, what an evil they have committed.' ** God censured them for this because they saw abomination and corruption perpetrated by the unjust among them and failed to order them to refrain out of greed for what they were getting from the corrupt or for fear of what they could suffer. God says: 'Fear not the people but fear me.' † He has also said: 'Faithful men and women are guardians over each other who order one another to do good deeds and who proscribe evil deeds.' ‡ God started with His order for good deeds and for prohibiting abomination as an ordinance because He knows that if this ordinance is performed then all the other ordinances, both easy and hard, will be set aright. The order for doing good deeds and refraining from evil deeds is a call for Islam, for averting injustice, for fighting the unjust, for sharing the taxes and the gains, for collecting alms and for giving them to those who rightly deserve them.

"As for you, who are a group known for its knowledge, who are mentioned favorably, who are known for good advice, who are revered by the honorable, honored by the weak, favored by those whom you hold under no obligation and whom you have done no favor, who invoke God to grant the needs of those who cannot get what they need and who walk with the prestige of kings and the dignity of the noble—as for you, have you not attained all this because it is hoped that you will achieve God's right, even though you have failed in achieving most of what is His due? You have taken the nation's right lightly and you have squandered the right of the poor. You have demanded that which you claim to be your right. You have spent no money, risked no life for Him Who created life and have fought no tribe for the sake of

* Al-Ma'idah 66.

** Al-Ma'idah 81.

† Al-Ma'idah, 47.

‡ Al-Tawbah, 72.

God. You implore God for His paradise, for becoming the neighbors of His messengers and for safety from His torture. I fear for you, you beseechers of God, I fear that His wrath will descend upon you because, with God's generosity, you have reached a position with which you have been favored. Those who know are aware that you do not honor God even though, by God, you are honored among his people. You see God's covenants disavowed and you are not alarmed whereas you get alarmed for the covenants of your fathers when the covenant of God's messenger is despised. The blind, the mute and the (sick) are neglected in the cities and you show no compassion. You do not work for what your position demands of you and you help nobody in your position. With flattery and praise, you have gained security from the unjust. God has proscribed all this to you and you ignore His order. Your catastrophe, if you can hear me, is the biggest because you have been vanquished from the position of the ulema and because the course of affairs and of laws must be set by the ulema who believe in God and who are faithful to His strictures and His permissibles. You have been robbed of this position and you have been robbed only because you are divided over what is right and because you disagree on the Sunna (sic) with its clear evidence. Had you endured hardship patiently and had you shouldered the responsibility for the sake of God, God's orders would have been returned to you, would have been issued by you and would have been referred to you. But you have enabled the unjust to seize your position and you have surrendered to them God's affairs and they are working with suspicion and indulging in lust. Your escape from death and your lust for life, which you are bound to leave, have enabled them to dominate. You have surrendered the weak to their hands and the people have become enslaved, oppressed and powerless. They rule with changing opinions all the time and they obey their shameful whims, following the evil and defying the Almighty. In every country, there is one of their loud-voiced preachers. The land is wide open and they have a free hand in it. People have become their slaves and are unable to repel their tyranny. They are obdurate tyrants who have no mercy for the weak and who do not know God. What an astounding condition, and why should I not be astounded when the land is dominated by an unjust tyrant and by a ruler who has no mercy for the faithful? God is the judge over our disputes and His sentence shall settle the dispute between us.

"God, you know that what we have done has not been in search of power or in pursuit of ephemeral things but to restore the landmarks of your religion, to reform affairs in you land, to restore security to the wronged among your people and to carry out your ordinances, your laws and your rules. If you do not support us and do us justice, the unjust and those who have sought to snuff the light of your prophet shall grow stronger. God is our reward, in Him we trust, on Him we rely and to Him we shall return."

Al-Husayn says: "Learn o people, from that with which God advised His holy men when He scorned al-Rabbaniyun and al-Ahbar." This speech is not intended solely for those whom the imam faced and addressed or to those present in Muna or the entire people of that age. It is a general address to all people in all times and all places. In its general and comprehensive nature, it is similar to God's repeated words in the Koran when He says, "O people." What is meant by the holy men in this paragraph are God's people who turn to God and who shoulder their well-known responsibility and not the imams, peace be upon them.

God says: "Al-Rabbaniyun and al-Ahbar have not ordered them to refrain from speaking evil and from unjust profit. What an evil have they committed!" This censure is not addressed exclusively to the Jewish and Christian learned men but also includes the ulema of Islam when they remain silent on the acts of injustice and tyranny that they witness. It is axiomatic that this censure is not confined to a former generation of ulema but includes the past, present and future generations equally. The imam, the amir of the faithful, cites the Koran to remind the ulema of Islam and to urge them to be alert and vigilant and to carry out their duty of ordering good deeds, proscribing evil, preventing injustice and refusing to condone it and keep silent on it. In his citing the venerable phrase, the imam points out two things:

1. The failure of the ulema and their silence is more harmful than that of others. The harm of an infraction or a sin committed by the ordinary person rarely exceeds the perpetrator whereas the infraction, sin, silence over injustice committed by the 'alim is of great harm to Islam in its entirety. When an 'alim carries out his duty in a perfect manner and when he speaks out at the right time, the benefit of his acts affect all of Islam also.

2. The imam attaches great significance to evil and to unjust profit, considering that they are among the abominable sins. Perhaps they are more serious than other sins and must be fought firmly. The words or statements made by the agencies of the unjust tyrants are perhaps more dangerous and harmful to Islam and its reputation than the devious policy and evil and illegal actions of these tyrants. In this Koran phrase, God censures whoever keeps silent and whoever does not refute or try to change evil statements. God calls for disowning whoever claims God's caliphate unrightfully or alleges that he represents religion in his actions and conduct which violate the laws of religion or who claims that he is just when justice disavows him altogether. The Hadith says: "If heresies appear in my nation, the 'alim must display his knowledge or else God's curse be upon him." An 'alim's confrontation of the heretics and his underlining God's laws and teachings which oppose the heretics, the unjust and the disobedient will enable the common people to discover the social corruption resulting from the injustices of the treacherous, profligate and infidel rulers and will make the people resist and boycott them and disobey their orders that emanate from positions of treachery, tyranny and corruption. In his intransigent and firm positions, the 'alim leads the process of proscribing abomination. Consequently, the

people in their entirety follow his lead in resisting the devious government. If the government does not turn away from its stray path, if it fails to abide by what God has ordered and if it resorts to the use of arms against the people, the people will then consider it a tyrant group that must be fought until it returns to God's orders.

Nowadays, you do not possess the power to fight the heresies of the rulers or to completely avert these evils. But why remain silent? These rulers are humiliating you so at least shout in their faces. Object, deny and refute them. To counter the means of publication and information that they possess, you must have on your side some of these means so that you may refute what they spread and disseminate and so that you may show the people that the justice that these rulers claim has nothing to do with the Islamic justice. The Islamic justice that God has given to the individual, the society and the family was written and legislated very precisely as of the first day. You must have a heard voice so that the future generations may not take your silence to mean a justification for the actions of the unjust, for their evil words, for their unjust profits and for their swallowing away the people's money unjustly.

How narrowminded are some people when they think that what is meant by illegal profit is cheating in weights and scales, God forbid, and when they never think of unjust profit in the other horrible ways that are occurring nowadays, such as embezzling the people's money and swallowing the entire treasury. These people are stealing our oil and selling it in the foreign monopoly markets under the name of investments and they thus attain illicit aggrandization. Foreign countries collaborate in producing and marketing our oil. In return, they give their agent rulers a small price which is again returned to these countries in every possible way. Should this money reach the treasury, then only God knows how, when and where it is spent and expended. This is unjust profit at the international level. It is horrible and dangerous abomination with nothing to surpass it. Consider the conditions of our society to realize the terrible forms of unfair profit. If an earthquake occurs somewhere in the country, the rulers gain enormous sums of money before the victims (get anything). In accordance with the treaties and agreements concluded by the treasonous rulers with the foreign countries and companies, many millions pour into the pockets of the rulers and other millions into the pockets of the foreigners, whereas the people get nothing out of the resources of their country. This is a form of unfair profit that is happening before our eyes and ears, and what we do not know is much more. In return for this, commercial agreements, oil prospecting and producing concessions, forest exploitation concessions, concessions on other natural resources, agreements on construction, communications and weapon purchases are concluded with the Western colonialists and with the communists.

We must fight unjust profits and the plundering of the national resources. This is a duty of all the people. But the ulema's task in this regard is heavier and more important. In this holy jihad and serious duty, we must lead the other people by virtue of our mission and position. Even though we are unable at present to resist, repel and punish the traitors, the profiteers and the plunderers of the people's money, we must try to reach these goals with all the legitimate means. At least we must not hesitate, while proceeding in our march to gain this ability, to underline the facts and to expose the stealing and plundering operations to which the country is exposed. If we attain power, we should not be content with improving the economy and ruling justly among the people but must make these traitors taste the worst torture for what they have done.

They burned al-Aqsa Mosque and we shouted: Let the traces of the crime remain. Meanwhile, the Shah opens a subscription in the banks to repair al-Aqsa Mosque. In this manner, he fills his pockets and coffers and increases his assets. After the mosque is repaired, he will have covered all traces of the Zionist crime.

These are catastrophes that have afflicted the nation and that have led it to this fate. Shouldn't the ulema express their opinion and shouldn't they shout, disown and resist? "Al-Rabbaniyun and al-Ahbar have not ordered them to refrain from speaking evil and from unjust profit."

The imam then says: "God censured them for this because they saw abomination and corruption perpetrated by the unjust among them and failed to order them to refrain out of greed for what they were getting from the corrupt or for fear of what they could suffer."

God censures those who fail to order good deeds and to proscribe evil out of fear or greed and says: "Fear not people but fear me." Why the fear? Let it be imprisonment, banishment or death. Holy men sacrifice themselves to gain God's approval: "Faithful men and women are guardians over each other who order one another to do good deeds and who proscribe evil deeds, who hold prayers, who pay the alms tax and who obey God and His messenger."

The imam then says: "God started with ordering good deeds and proscribing evil deeds as his ordinance because He knows that if this ordinance is performed, then all the other ordinances, both easy and hard, will be set aright. This is because ordering good deeds and proscribing evil deeds is a call for Islam, for repelling injustice, for fighting the unjust, for sharing profits and gains and for collecting alms and giving them to those who deserve them." To achieve these great things, and not for the trivialities that we see and hear every day, Islam legislated the order for doing good deeds and proscribing evil deeds, even though we must disavow and deter such trivialities.

What harm would there be if the ulema rise in unison against tyranny? What harm would it do them if they protest and send cables from all part of the Moslem world denouncing the unjust acts committed by the authorities? These authorities would back down under the impact of the enormous pressure because they are cowardly, as I know them to be. But having discerned weakness in us, these authorities have done whatever they please.

When the ulema were united and backed by the people in all parts of the country, the government backed down on its position to a certain degree. It then proceeded to sow the seed of division and conflict among us. As a result, the government became daring and proceeded to do whatever they wanted and to choose that which no good people would have anything to do with.

Ordering good deeds and proscribing evil deeds is a call for Islam for fighting injustice and resisting the unjust. Therefore, most ordering and proscribing must be directed at those who tamper with people's lives, money and properties. Some acts of embezzlement of donations for aiding victims of floods and earthquakes may even surface in the newspapers. One of (Malayir's) ulema has said: We sent a truckload of shrouds to the victims of an accident that claimed many lives. However, the officials tried to prevent us from delivering the shrouds and wanted to appropriate them! The command ordering good deeds and proscribing evil ones has come for this kind and for similar evils.

Now I ask You: Should we not take the imam's words "O people" into consideration? Aren't we part of the people? Doesn't the address include us? Were the imam's speeches addressed exclusively to his friends and contemporaries? I have already said that the teachings of the imams are like the teachings of the Koran. They are not teachings meant for one generation exclusively but are teachings that are intended for all people in all ages and in all countries and must be implemented and followed until the day of resurrection. As al-Ahbar and al-Rabbaniyun are censured for their unjustifiable silence, so are the ulema when they keep silent on

90

Portrait of the Ayatollah Ruhollah Khomeini shortly before his arrest in July 1963. After making an inflammatory speech to a crowd of more than 100,000 in Qum, the Ayatollah was arrested and imprisoned by the Shah. In 1964 he was released and exiled to Iraq. "All the problems besetting Iran and other Islamic nations are the doing of the aliens of the United States," he said at that time. (Wide World Photos)

The residential palace of the former Shah, Mohammed Riza Pahlavi, before the revolution. The Shah and Empress Farah lived in regal splendor in the white palace at Saadabad, Tehran. The personal fortune amassed by the Shah and his family is estimated at more than one billion dollars. (Wide World Photos)

The Ayatollah at prayer. Expelled from Iraq on October 6, 1978, Khomeini took up residence in France at the small town of Neauphle-le-Chateau just outside of Paris. There, with a small group of followers, he received daily reports on the growing unrest in Iran. Using long-distance telephone connections with Tehran, he was able to arrange meetings and organize demonstrations among the clergy and his followers. (Wide World Photos)

After months of unrest, it appeared in mid-January that peace had returned to Iran. Tehran University was reopened on January 13 and students marched in the streets in peaceful demonstrations. Iranian soldiers standing guard were rewarded by the students with gifts of carnations. (Wide World Photos)

On January 16, 1979, Khomeini received news that the Shah had left Iran. Addressing supporters outside his residence in Neauphle-le-Chateau, the Ayatollah said, "The Shah's departure is the first step toward ending fifty years of the Pahlavi dynasty in Iran." Two weeks later Khomeini would make his entry into Tehran. (Wide World Photos)

With news that the Shah had left the country, crowds in Tehran poured into the streets in jubilant celebration. Within days Iranians were demanding the return and trial of the deposed monarch for crimes committed during his reign. One student holds a WANTED poster of Shah Riza Pahlavi. (Wide World Photos)

Two days after the Shah's departure from Iran Khomeini was visited at his retreat in France by PLO leader Yasser Arafat. The meeting ended amicably, with handshakes and kisses. Khomeini's son, Ahmad, has his hand on Arafat's shoulder. (Wide World Photos)

Another visitor to Khomeini's house at Neauphle-le-Chateau was former Attorney General Ramsey Clark. After the meeting on January 22, Clark shakes hands with the Ayatollah's son-in-law, Shahab Eshraghi. Months later, when the United States Embassy was taken over, Clark offered to negotiate on behalf of the hostages, but was turned down by Khomeini. (Wide World Photos)

In Iran crowds anticipated the return of the Ayatollah with massive demonstrations. On January 22 young Moslem women marched through the streets of Tehran chanting "God Is Great" and carrying portraits of Khomeini. Earlier in the day a supporter was killed during demonstrations. (Wide World Photos)

To prevent the Ayatollah's return, the Iranian army closed all airports and grounded the national airline. At a news conference in France on January 25 Khomeini announced the postponement of his return. Reaction in Iran was immediate and violent. (Wide World Photos)

Attempting to storm police headquarters on January 28, rioters were shot down by army and police marksmen stationed on the rooftops. In two days of bloody riots, thirty-seven were killed and more than two hundred demonstrators wounded. The riots were touched off when airports were closed to prevent the Ayatollah's return. (Wide World Photos)

Freshly dug graves hold the bodies of victims of the January 28 riots. The day of the funeral, there were further demonstrations and marches in Tehran. In the wake of protests the airport in Tehran was reopened. (Wide World Photos)

A few hours before his departure from France, Ayatollah Ruhollah Khomeini is surrounded by well-wishers. Followers form a human chain to keep back the crowd as he leaves his residence at Neauphle-le-Chateau. With his departure on January 31 Khomeini ended his four-month stay in France. (Wide World Photos)

The Ayatollah flew from Charles de Gaulle Airport in France to Tehran in a chartered Air France 747 jetliner. Millions of followers greeted him upon his arrival, which ended nearly fifteen years of exile from Iran. (Wide World Photos)

His years of exile over, Ayatollah Ruhollah Khomeini descends the gangway at Tehran airport. He is heavily guarded by police carrying submachine guns. Behind him is the Ayatollah's son, Ahmad. (Wide World Photos)

The Ayatollah, heavily guarded, enters the car that will take him to Behesht Zahra cemetery outside Tehran. In Tehran, Iranians turned out en masse to hear him speak. (Wide World Photos)

Hundreds of thousands of Iranians gathered to hear Khomeini's first speech to the nation. Addressing the crowd at Behesht Zahra cemetery, Khomeini commemorated the "martyrs" who fell in the Islamic struggle against the Shah. (Wide World Photos)

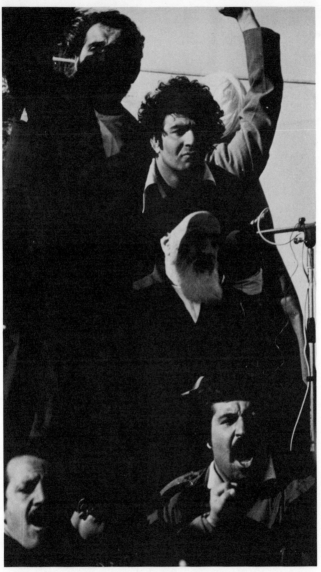

Supporters of the Ayatollah responded with raised arms and clenched fists. Days before, victims of demonstrations in Tehran were buried at the cemetery, amid demonstrations of grief. (Wide World Photos)

At a news conference in Tehran Khomeini announced that Premier Mehdi Bazargan would continue in his post under the new regime. Bazargan later resigned in protest at Khomeini's escalating, anti-American campaign. (Wide World Photos)

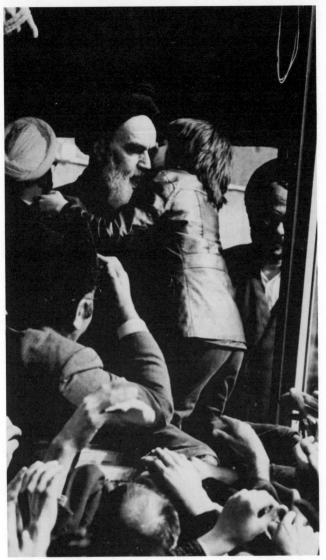

Khomeini took up residence in the holy city of Qum just outside Tehran, where he was greeted daily by crowds of well-wishers. Here a young boy welcomes the Ayatollah with a kiss on the cheek as the religious leader greets supporters. (Wide World Photos)

On February 13, just two weeks after the Ayatollah's return, many Iranian rebels turned in their weapons at his request. Though Khomeini was widely supported by the Shiite sect of Moslems, his regime has been troubled by leftists, Kurdish rebels, and rival religious leaders. (Wide World Photos)

Officials from the Shah's government were summarily tried and executed in the months following Khomeini's return. Here the former Iranian premier Amir Abass pleads for his life during a Revolutionary Court hearing on March 16. Abass was later executed. (Wide World Photos)

Police and military officials were tried and shot for acts carried out under the Shah. This military police sergeant, convicted of killing anti-Shah demonstrators, was executed by a Revolutionary Committee firing squad. (Wide World Photos)

oppression and when they fail to disown it and try to change it with all the power they possess.

The imam continues to address the people and to censure them, saying: "The blind, the mute and the sick are neglected in the cities and you have no compassion for them." Do you think that all that the information media say is true? Go to the villages and the rural areas and you will hardly find a single clinic in every one hundred or two hundred villages! They have not thought of the starved and of the naked, they have not allowed them to think and they have not permitted Islam to solve their problem. Islam, as you know well, solved the problem of poverty and decided at the very outset that "the alms are for the poor." Islam arranged and organized this but they are not allowing Islam to get Islam to get to the Moslems in any way.

The nation is living in a state of hardship while the authorities go on with their extravagant spending and with increasing taxes. They purchase the Phantom aircraft so that the Israelis may be trained on them. Considering that Israel is in a state of war with the Moslems, then whoever helps and supports it is in turn in a state of war with the Moslems. The Israeli influence in our country has reached an unbearable extent and the Israelis use our lands for their bases and as their markets, and this is something that will gradually lead to the decline of the Moslem markets.

Thus, you see that the entire address is concerned with God's ulema generally and not just the imams, may peace be upon them, because the ulema of Islam are learned men who know about God, who uphold His strictures and who are faithful to His permissibles and His prohibitions.

When the imam says "the course of affairs is at the hands of the ulema who know God and who are faithful to His permissibles and His prohibitions," he does not mean the ulema of that age in particular but the ulema of an entire nation. If the ulema are faithful to the permissible and the prohibited and if they combine justice and good conduct with their knowledge, then they can take charge of affairs, establish the strictures and set up the religious system, without misery, injustice or obstruction of the laws.

This Hadith supports our discussion. Were it not for weak quotation, we would consider it the strongest proof of our issue, that is if we don't go as far as saying that its contents indicate that it did truly emanate from the infallible one [Imam al-Husayn].

Here we end our discussion of the issue of the governance of the jurisprudent. We need not dwell on the subsidiaries of the issue, such as outlining how taxes are to be collected and strictures are to be established. There are subsidiary issues for which this discussion is not the place. We have discussed the essence of the issue, namely the governance of the jurisprudent of the Islamic government. It has become evident to us that what was acknowledged for the prophet and the imams is also acknowledged for the jurisprudent. There is no doubt about this issue and there is nothing new that we have innovated. The issue was discussed from the beginning.

You have the ruling of the departed al-Mirza al-Shirazi prohibiting tobacco (smoking). His ruling emanated from the jurisprudent's position of general governance over the people and over the other jurisprudents. Iran's jurisprudents, except for a few of them, adhered to this ruling. Al-Shirazi's ruling was not a ruling for the settlement of a dispute or a disagreement between two sides but was a governance ruling which took into consideration the interests of the Moslems according to the times and to the prevailing conditions. With the disappearance of those conditions, the ruling ceased.

When the late Mirza Muhammad Taqui al-Shirazi issued his interpretation on the jihad—defense—his ruling emanated from the position of his government and from his legitimate public governance.

I have already told you that the late al-Niraqi believes that all the prophet's affairs are acknowledged for the jurisprudents, except for whatever was excluded of his private affairs. The departed Shaykh al-Na'ini said: "All this issue is concluded from 'Umar ibn Hanzalah's concurrence."

In any case, the issue is not new and we have been content with bringing the subject of the legitimate government closer to the minds of the esteemed gentlemen. In obedience to God's order and to what was said by his prophet, we have explained the issues strongly needed in our life. This is an issue which many people have understood and of which they have been convinced.

We have presented the issue for discussion and the future generations must pursue it more deeply with resolution, firmness and a spirit of persistence that knows no despair. They will succeed, God willing, in forming the government and organizing other affairs through the exchange of sincere, objective and unbiased opinions. The affairs of the Moslem government will, God willing, be taken over by trustworthy, knowledgeable, experienced and wise people with a firm faith in the creed and the hands of the traitors will be cut off and prevented from reaching the government, the homeland or the treasury. God is capable of giving them the victory.

Path of Struggle for Forming Islamic Government

We must exert serious efforts to form the Islamic government and we must begin our work with propaganda activity and must develop this activity. In the entire world and throughout the ages, ideas emerged through interaction among a number of people, then came designs and planning and then started the work and the attempt to spread and disseminate the ideas in order to persuade other people gradually. Then such people gained influence in government from within to change it in the way those ideas and their advocated wanted the government to be or the advocates of the ideas launched their assault from outside government to uproot it and to replace it by a government built on the basis of such ideas.

Ideas begin small and then grow, then people rally behind them, they gain strength and take charge of affairs ultimately. Strength has not been, as you can see, the ally of ideas as of the first day. In all this, the peole with all their forces must be taken as a firm base on which to rely and depend. Ceaseless efforts must also be exerted to enlighten the people, to expose the criminal plans and to expose the deviation existing among the temporal authorities. The masses, all the masses, are thus polarized gradually and the goal is then achieved.

You do not presently possess a state or any army but you can advocate because your enemy has not been able to rob you of your ability to preach, guide and inform. In addition to explaining worship issues, you must also explain to the people the political issues of Islam and its judiciary, penal, economic and social laws. Use this as the pivot of your work. We must seek as of this moment to lay down the cornerstone of the legitimate Islamic state and must advocate and disseminate ideas, issue instructions, win supporters and backers and create waves of alert guidance and coordinated direction of the masses so that mass reaction may ensue and in its wake, the masses of enlightened Moslems who cling tp their religion will be fully ready to undertake the tasks of forming the Islamic government.

The jurisprudents must explain the Islamic issues, laws and systems and must bring them closer to the minds of the people so as to create a fertile soil on which the Islamic rules and laws will survive. As you have already learned, the prophet's Hadith says "and they teach them to the people."

Our responsibility today, and at a time when all the forces of colonialism and its agents, the treasonous rulers, Zionism and atheistic materialism are collaborating to distort Islam, is heavier than ever before. Here we see the Jews tampering with the Koran and distorting its phrases in new editions which they have published in the occupied territories and other parts. We must expose this treachery and must shout at the top of our voices so that we may make the people realize that the Jews and their foreign masters seek to snare Islam and pave the way for Jews to dominate thie entire world. The worst that can be feared is that they achieve their goals in their special ways. Because of our weakness, we may awaken one day to find a Jewish ruler ruling our country, God forbid. On the other hand, some orientalists have worked with the colonialist institutions and both have worked hand in hand to distort and destroy the facts of Islam. The colonialist missionaries are exerting serious efforts to deceive our youths in all parts of the country with their lies and to lead them away from us. I am not saying that they are trying to Christianize or Judaize the youths. It is enough that they are working to corrupt them and to make them disavow religion and to become indifferent. It is enough for colonialism that this success and other successes like it be achieved.

Christian, Jewish and Baha'i missionary centers are spread in Tehran to deceive people and to lead them away from the teachings and principles of religion. Isn't it a duty to destroy these centers? Is it enough for us to own al-Najaf, which we do not own? Should we stay in Qum to increase the ceremonies of mourning or should we work with utter firmness and resolution to enlighten the people? You, the youths of the religious centers, be active and work to revive the order of your God and to preserve his laws. You, the young generation, unite and work and "God, His prophet and the faithful will see your works." Be complete, leave trivialities alone, turn away from superficialities and shoulder your responsibilities. Help and rescue Islam because Islam is crying for your help. Save the Moslems from the dangers engulfing them. Here they (Christians and Jews) are killing Islam in the name of religion and in the name of the prophet. Their missionaries, who are the lackeys of colonialism, have spread throughout the country, have invaded villages, rural areas and subdistricts and have aimed their efforts at children; juveniles and youths, who are the hope of Islam, and have misled them. Rise to help these misled young people. Rescue them and help them. You must disseminate your knowledge because the praise and glorification given to ulema (learned men) is due to the fact they teach others and save them from falsehood. You must exert utmost efforts to convey the concepts and laws of Islam to the people generally. We must lift the screen that the enemies have lowered over Islam and we must remove from Islam the ambiguity that they have attached to it. Without this, we will be destined not to achieve any progress. We must advise each other and advise the others to remove this fabricated ambiguity and suspicion that the enemies have injected into the people, even the educated among them, throughout long centuries. We recommend that the young generation explain to all other generations the international character of Islam, its social legislations and the laws it contains and that they speak out on what Islam has legislated concerning the issue of government so that people may learn what Islam is and what laws it has brought.

The religious academies in Qum, Khurasan and everywhere must guide people to the path of Islam and must present the ideas of Islam in the sunlight. People are ignorant of Islam and know almost nothing about it. You yourselves must acquaint them with your creed and with how your government should be. You must familiarize the entire world with these matters and must disseminate them among college people in particular because they are more enlightened than others. Be confident that good results will emanate from all this and that Islam will be welcomed ardently by college people. College people are most hostile to repression, agentry, treason, the plundering of wealth and resources and unjust gains and they will find in Islam— whose teachings in the sphere of govenment, the judiciary, economy and social affairs you will convey to them—traits that will attract them to it. These college people are extending their hands to al-Najag, seeking to understand the facts of their religion. Does it behoove us to remain silent and idle until these college people awaken us from our slumber and compel us to perform our duty and play our role in ordering good deeds and proscribing evil deeds? Isn't it a disgrace for us to neglect the matter until we are faced with youths from Europe who have formed an Islamic coalition through which they have asked us for cultural, directional and guidance aid?

We must remind people of what the government used to be at the outset of Islam. We must tell them that the judiciary bench used to be located in the corner of a mosque when the Moslem countries grew and included Iran, Egypt, Hejaz, Yemen and other places. When, unfortunately, matters were taken over by others, the legal succession and the government turned into a futile monarchy. We must remind them of all this and stress the characteristics of the government that we intend to form. We must outline the qualities of the ruler, his powers, his duties and his morals. The nation's leader and amir deterred his brother 'Aqil and heated an iron with which to punish him so that he may not covet the monies of the Moslems. He censured his daughter when she borrowed a necklace from the treasury and said: "Were you not (naked and guaranteed), you would be the first Hashimite woman to have her hand cut off." He then returned the necklace to the treasury house. This is the ruler that we want. For this let those who exert their efforts work and for this let the rivals compete. We want a ruler who does not order us to do anything before preceding us to doing it and who does not prevent us from anything before he personally refrains from it. We want him to treat us equally in judiciary matters and in the spheres of justice. We want him to treat the people equally in their rights and their duties without discrimination or favors. We want him to rule by what is right, be it for him or against him. We want a ruler who does not allow himself, his family and his kinsmen to be a burden to the people. We want a ruler who disowns his son if he steals, who whips and stones his relative if he commits adultery and who punishes his brother and sister when they engage in trading tons of heroin as he punishes those who smuggle a small quantity of heroin.

Meetings for Spreading the Principles

Many of the worship laws result in social and political services. The worship practices of Islam are usually a twin to its policies and its social measures. The group prayer, for example, the pilgrimage meeting and the Friday prayers lead, in addition to their moral and emotional impact, to political consequences and effects. Islam established these gatherings, urged people to attend them and made it obligatory to attend some of them so that religious knowledge and fraternal feelings may spread, so that the bonds of acquaintance and friendship among people may grow stronger, so that thoughts may grow, develop and interact and so that social and political problems and their solutions may be discussed.

In non-Moslem countries, millions of the country's resources and budget are spent for holding such meetings and when they are held, they are mostly superficial meetings that lack the element of purity, goodwill and the fraternity prevailing among people in their Islamic meetings. Consequently, such meetings do not end up with the fruitful results that our Islamic meetings lead to. Islam has created intrinsic incentives and motives that make performing the pilgrimage one of life's dearest wishes and that make people automatically attend these meetings and participate with utter joy and pleasure in Friday prayers and in holidays. All we have to do is to consider such meetings golden opportunities to serve the principle and the creed and to explain in them the beliefs, the laws and the rules publicly, and to the largest number of people possible. We must benefit from the pilgrimage season and to reap from it the best fruits by calling for unity and for making Islam ruler among all the people. We must discuss our problems and must discover the fundamental solutions drawn up for them by Islam. We must try to liberate the lands of the Moslems in Palestine and other places. We find that in the early age of Islam, the Moslems reaped the best fruits from their gatherings, Friday prayers, holidays and pilgrimages. The sermons delivered on Fridays, holidays and other occasions were not confined to promises of heaven and threats of hell and to light or heavy phrases of the Koran, as we witness today. The sermons reached in their influence and inspiration the extent of preparing the people to fight with utter courage and valor and even made people proceed to battlefronts from the yards of mosques without any fear of poverty, sickness, death or loss because people feared God alone and nobody else. Victory and conquests are written for such people. Look at the speeches of the amir of the faithful to realize that they drove people to the fields of jihad and made them sacrifice and that these speeches formulated the most successful solutions for people's problems in this life.

Had Friday prayers continued until our day with their sermons, their zeal, their spirit and their spheres of thought, we would not have ended in what you see. We must seek to revive these meetings and to utilize them for guidance, direction, enlightenment and for leading toward reform and success. The Islamic thoughts will thus be able to expand at the broadest level and to rise to levels that nothing else tops.

New "Ashura"

As you observe the sad anniversary of "Ashura" (Imam al-Husayn's martyrdom on hands of Ommiad's in Karbala' in year sixty of the Hegira) and as you never relinquish it, let the catastrophes that have afflicted the religion of Islam from the first day and until the present day be a new "Ashbura"whose anniversary you observe constantly. If you speak about Islam with utter sincerity and if you stress to the

99

people its social fundaments, laws, rules and systems, people will welcome and follow this religion. God knows that Islam lovers are many but they are ignorant of most of its laws. I have tried this myself. When I make a speech I feel a change in the people and I feel the impact on them because they are displeased with the condition under which they live. Fear of the tyrants is filling their hearts and they are in the direct need of people who speak courageously and firmly. Sons of Islam, be strong and firm in explaining your cause to the people so that you may defeat your enemy with all his weapons, troops and guards. Highlight the facts to the people and urge them. Inject the spirit of jihad in the market and street people, in the worker, the peasant and the university man. All will rise for the jihad. All demand freedom, independence, happiness and dignity. Make the teachings of Islam available to all, because Islam is for all, and you will find that it will lead them to the path, light their way, correct their thoughts and beliefs and will make them offer and sacrifice so that the agencies of the policy of tyranny and colonialism may be destroyed and so that the Islamic government may rise on firm foundations.

The jurisprudents (the strongholds of Islam) must expound to people the true Islamic beliefs, laws and the methods of jihad and struggle and must lead the people who will follow them automatically if they discern in them worthiness, sincerity and self-denial. In such a case, the loss of such ulema will constitute to the people a major tragedy that leaves a terrible void in the life of the people and will create in Islam a gap that nothing can fill. Such a void and gap is not caused by the loss of myself or people like me who sit in a corner of their house but by the loss of people like Imam al-Husayn and the imams that followed him. People also felt the loss of al-Khawajah Nasir-al-Din al-Tusi, al-'Allamah and other people like them who rendered Islam great services. As for me and you, what have we offered Islam that the true Hadith may apply to us? There is no void when a thousand of the likes of us die because our life is a void and no gap will emerge in Islam when a thousand like us die because our life, as it is, may be a gap in Islam that must be filled with others.

Long-range Resistance

We do not expect our instructions and efforts to bear fruit in a short time because laying down the foundations of the Islamic government requires a long time and exhaustive efforts. We see many wisemen who lay down a stone so that the others may build an edifice over it, even if after two hundred years.

An old man planting a seedling was asked about the fruit of his work which he would not see and he replied: Others before us planted and we have eaten and we plant so others may eat. If our efforts will bring no fruit until another generation, then this must not discourage us because rendering services to mankind should not be on the basis of individual interest but on the basis of the general interest of the Moslems. Had the master of the martyrs (al-Husayn) who sacrificed everything he owned proceeded on the basis of individualistic thinking, he would have put his hand in their (the enemies') hands and would have settled everything. Such an end was one of the dearest wishes of the Ommiads. But al-Husayn was thinking of Islam and the Moslems and their future generations in the long run. His uprising and his sacrifice and struggle were for the purpose of disseminating Islam and of expounding its political laws and its social rules among the people.

In a previously cited quotation from Imam al-Sadiqu, you find that despite the conditions engulfing him and forcing him into dissimulation and despite his loss of authority he still explained issues to the Moslems, appointed for them judges and rulers and ordered Moslems to refer to them to settle their disputes. Great men plan for future generations and are not saddened not to see the effects of their plans as long as the future is certain to produce results and fruits. Such men do not feel despair even in the humiliation of captivity and in the bowels of prisons. For the triumph of great goals, great men plan in prisons for the happiness of future generations and attaining what they want is not their sole concern. Many movements and revivals take their final form after preparations that may date back to two hundred or three hundred years sometimes.

Imam al-Sadiq was not content with drawing up the broad lines of the Islamic government or state but also appointed and installed a ruler. Naturally, he did not mean the appointment to be for the age in which he lived because he was the imam and the legitimate ruler. He was considering the future generations and he was thinking more of his nation than of himself and his person. He wanted to reform people, all the people, and the world, all the world, under the canopy of the just Islamic law. He appointed those fit for rule so that when conditions improve and when matters return to normal, people would find no difficulty and no dilemma as to who would occupy the post of ruler, judge and leader of the people.

Religion in its essence, especially the Shiite creed, and all religions started as teachings. Because of the resolution, firmness and constancy of the rulers, the faith advanced in steady steps.

Moses was a shepherd and a guard for long years. When he was entrusted with confronting Pharaoh, there was nobody to help him. With his abilities, qualities and powers, he was able to defeat Pharaoh's rule with his staff. Do not imagine that if Moses' staff was in my hand or in the hand of any of you it would do anything because we do not have Moses' wisdom, his determination and his serious concentration on his work. This is not available to everybody. When the message was revealed to God's messenger, the only source of power he had was nothing more than a child not yet ten years of age, namely 'Ali ibn Abi Talib, and an old woman, namely his wife Khadijah. They believed in him and supported and helped him. The other people harmed and opposed him and branded him as a liar. But despair found no way to the hearts of the prophet and of his two supporters. They remained steadfast, patient and resolute until God's word surged. The false were defeated and Islam struck its roots east and west and no less than seven hundred million people believe in it nowadays.

The Shiite sect started from the zero point. When the prophet laid down the foundation of the succession, he was met with derision and ridicule. The prophet gathered his people, feasted them and told them among other things: "Who will be my successor, my guardian and my minister over this matter? Only 'Ali, who had not come of age yet, rose. At that point, one of them said to Abi Talib ('Ali's father): Your nephew wants you to listen to and obey your son!"

In Ghadir Khamm during the farewell (last) pilgrimage, the prophet appointed 'Ali a ruler after him. Since then, disagreement started to appear. Had the prophet appointed the amir of the faithful as an interpreter and an expounder of the Koran and of the laws only, nobody would have opposed 'Ali. But 'Ali was opposed and was fought because he became the legitimate ruler in charge of the people's and the country's affairs. If you stay in your homes, then you have nothing to fear. But the day you want to emerge in society as an element of reform or change with all the power you possess, war will be declared on you. Because of the stances of the imams and of their Shi'ite sect toward the theory of government and administration in Islam, they suffered and continue to suffer harm, misfortunes and hardship but they have not despaired and hope still fills their hearts. The number of Shiites is increasing and nowadays they number nearly two hundred million.

Reform of Religious Authorities

Leading the nation toward reform and knowing the true face of Islam requires the ulema and the bearers of the laws to be righteous, in the sense that their teaching efforts, their self-reliance and their confidence must be integrated. They must avoid idleness, weakness and withdrawal. They must erase from among people the traces of the falsehood disseminated amongst them, must polish the petrified and repulsive ideas harbored by some of us and must oust from our ranks and must expose and unveil the jurisprudents of the palaces who have sold their religion for the world of the others.

Eliminating Traces of Intellectual and Moral Colonialist Aggression

For centuries, the agents of colonialism and the educational and political agencies have injected their poisons into the people's minds and ethics until they corrupted them. The people have become suspicious of us because of these poisons. Our religious academies and councils need to be reformed. The sick ideas coming from abroad must also be uprooted and every form of corruption, evil and deviation in society must be fought.

We notice the presence among our ranks of people who are influenced by these poisons and we find some of these people whispering to each other: These actions have not been created for us and we have not been created for them. What do we have to do with all this? We only beseech God and explain the issues. This logic is the result of what the foreigners have been implanting in the minds of the people for hundreds of years and this is what makes the hearts in al-Najaf, Qum and Khurasan weak, feeble, and untrue to the faith. Their argument in all this is: This is none of our business.

These are wrong ideas. Do the actual rulers have greater capabilities and talents than we do? Who among them is worthy of leading and guiding the people? Aren't some of them illiterate? Where was the ruler of Hejaz educated? Wasn't Rida Khan * an ignorant man? History tells us about ignorant rulers who governed people unworthily and without any qualifications. What education did Harun al-Rashid and those before and after him have?

We must benefit from people with scientific and technical specialization in connection with statistical, administrative and organizational works. As for the supreme state administration and for spreading justice, providing security, establishing just social relations, for judiciary affairs and for dispensing justice among the people, this is the jurisdiction of the jurisprudent and the thing on which the jurisprudent spends all his life. The jurisprudent possesses that which safeguards the people's freedom, independence and progress within a straight policy in which foreigners have no influence and which does not swerve to the right or to the left.

Break away from your isolation and complete your academic and guidance programs and face hardships for this. Plan for the Islamic government, project your plans and unite for this purpose with whomever demands freedom and independence because you will certainly attain you goals. Rely on yourselves. Your experience and your expertise will grow on the path of your struggle which scares and terrifies colonialism. I am confident that you are capable of running the government when the foundation of tyranny, injustice and aggression are destroyed. All the laws and regulations you need are present in our Islam, whether the laws and regulations pertaining to state management, taxes, rights,

* Father of the present Shah.

penalties or to other issues. You need no new legislation. You must implement what has already been legislated for you. This saves you a lot of time and effort and spares you the need of borrowing laws from the east or the west. Everything is, God be thanked, ready to be used. All that remains is for you to organize the ministries, their jurisdictions, their activities and their tasks. All this can be done by specialists very rapidly. It is fortunate that the Moslem peoples are with you and that the masses follow you and take your lead. You will grow stronger. All we need is Moses' staff and 'Ali ibn Abi Talib's sword and their mighty will. If we resolve to set up an Islamic rule, we will get Moses' staff and 'Ali ibn Abi Talib's sword also.

Yes, there are among us negligent and obscure individuals who master almost nothing, who write no scientific paper, who never open their mouths with a word of guidance and who hardly understand a conversation on life's affairs. Such individuals have succumbed to the notion that they have no capability as a result of what the agents have disseminated among us, things like: What concern of yours is this? Pay attention to your studies and go to your school. Here we are now unable to persuade some of us of the mistake they have committed through the isolation, negligence and indifference toward the affairs of the Moslems that they have developed.

Explain to the people the programs of the Islamic government. Make this clear to the entire world and perhaps the rulers and leaders of the Moslems will be convinced by the soundness of such programs and will follow them. We are not competing with them for seats of power and we will leave those of them who follow and who sincerely implement the programs in their positions.

We must form a faithful government which the people can depend on and trust and to which they surrender their affairs. We want those who will shoulder the task faithfully and sincerely so that people may live under their rule safely. God knows that your competence and worthiness to take

106

charge of people's affairs are no less than those of the others, except that we cannot kill unjustly and cannot commit injustice and tyranny because this is not within our powers.

When I was in jail in Iran, and al-Sayyid al-Qummi, may God protect him, who is still in jail was with me, one of the Iranian statesmen told me: "Politics are malice, falsehood and hypocrisy. Leave this for us." This is true. If policy means only these things, then it is theirs in this sense. But politics in Islam and politics to the imams, who are the managers of people as al-Ziyarah (visit) phrase in the Koran says, do not mean what that man said. That man wanted to deceive and mislead us. On the following day, the press appeared to declare that "agreement and understanding have been reached that clergymen will not interfere in politics from now on." After I was released, I ascended the pulpit and denied the press reports that were published at the time and said: "The man is lying. Any of our men who say this must be banished from the country."

These people, as you can see, have made your believe that politics are malice, trickery and slyness to divert your attention from politics and to tamper with the nation's affairs as they wish and to implement what they want on the instructions of their British and American masters whose influence have escalated in our country recently.

While I was in Hamadan, a distinguished man came to me with a map bearing red marks indicating the locations of the mineral wealth stored under our land. The foreign experts had found out where the gold is deposited, where copper is found and where oil is present. They probed among us and became certain that the only obstacle standing in the way of achieving their ambitions was the strong spiritualism and the teachings of the orthodox religion. Those enemies became aware of the capabilities latent in Islam and attached major importance to them. History taught them that Islam opened the doors of Europe and ruled it for a long time. Therefore, a realistic Islam is incompatible with what they want. On the other hand, they felt that the true ulema cannot condone them or march in their bandwagon. Because of all this, their attempts focused as of the first day on eliminating this obstacle from their path and on undermining the importance of Islam and of spiritualism with all the propaganda means at their disposal. Thus, you find many people who view Islam as no more than several Shari'a issues and you find others who do not think well of the ulema. The agents of colonialism have tried to accuse and defame the ulema and some of them have gone as far as announcing with utter impudence and shamelessness that "600 of al-Najaf and Iran ulemas were working for the British" and that "Shaykh al-Ansari used to collect bimonthly wages from them." The agent who announced this relies on documents of the British Ministry of Foreign Affairs in India. How eager is colonialism to fabricate these accusations?

On the other hand, they have done their utmost to undermine the importance of Islam and to restrict its duties and the tasks of the jurisprudents and the ulema in charge of its affairs. They have restricted these duties to explaining issues, to making sermons and to giving guidance. Some naive people have believed them and have unwittingly lost their way. I tell you: These defamatory accusations and these efforts are aimed against the country's independence and against its resources.

All the colonialist establishments have whispered in the ears of the people that religion is incompatible with politics. Spiritualism is not required and should not interfere in social affairs. The ulema have no right to exert efforts to decide the nation's destiny. It is very regrettable that some of us have believed these falsehoods. With such belief, the greatest wish of which the colonialists were dreaming has been realized.

Look at the religious authorities and you will find clearly the impact and results of this propaganda. There are the idle who have no will and there are the lazy who are content with invocation, praise and discussion of the Shari'a issues, as if they were created for nothing else. What can be felt in this atmosphere and under the impact of these traces and effects is the following: "Speaking out is incompatible with the position of the ulema. It behooves a religious interpreter not to speak and it behooves him to remain silent and to be content with the words: There is no god but God and with very few other words." This is wrong and it is in violation of the noble Sunna. God praises eloquence in al-Ruhman (the compassionate) phrase of the Koran when He, may He be praised, says: "God taught him eloquence." God thus holds his servants obliged for His teaching them eloquence and reminds them of His bestowing on them this blessing of learning. Eloquence is good for teaching people their true beliefs and the laws of their religion and for leading them to the shore of Islam. The prophet and the amir of the faithful were the greatest princes of eloquence.

Reforming Those Who Claim Holiness

There are those among us who believe the silly ideas that the enemies disseminate among us, some of which we have just mentioned and which perpetuate colonialism and foreign influence. These silly people are called holy men whereas in fact they are no holy men who claim holiness and who pretend to be holy. We must reform these people and must define our position toward them because they prevent us from achieving reform, progress and revival.

The late Ayatollah al-Barujardi, Ayatollah al-Hijjah, Ayatollah al-Sadr and Ayatollah al-Khunsari * met in my home once to discuss an important political matter. I asked them to define their positions toward those who claim holiness stupidly and to consider them internal enemies because these people are not concerned with what is happening and because they prevent the real ulema from assuming power and taking charge of affairs. These people deal the biggest

* Major Shiite Authorities.

blow to Islam, constitute the biggest danger to it and display it in the most distorted form. There are many such people in al-Najaf, Qum and Khurasan * and they have influence over the naive and silly people like them. These people who claim holiness oppose whoever speaks loudly to the people to awaken them from the deep slumber into which they have fallen. These claimants urge people to be lazy and tardy and they oppose whoever resists and fights the influence of the British and the Americans.

We must first advise such people to abandon their erroneous way, must draw their attention to the danger surrounding Islam and the Moslems and must open their eyes wide to the Zionist danger and to the Anglo-American (colonialism) that supplies the Israeli entity with the mainstays of life. Do not turn off the light and submerge yourselves in darkness, as the Christians did before you. Their debate on the trinity, the hypostases and on the father and the son preoccupied them and left them with nothing else. Beware and look at the facts as they are. Discuss the life issues of today and of the future.

In your present situation, do you expect the angels to put their wings under your feet in veneration for you? Are not the angels preoccupied with other things? The angels put their wings under the feet of the amir of the faithful because of his precedence, his service and his spreading Islam throughout the world. The angles obey him and so do people, even his enemies, because they obey right sitting or standing, speaking or silent, praying or fighting. What part of this veneration do you deserve? Nothing.

We should thus address those who claim holiness. If reminding is any use, then this is what we want. Otherwise, we will bring them to a different account and will have a different position toward them.

---

* They contain major religious centers and universities.

Purging Religious Centers

These religious and scientific centers, where theology and religious leadership are taught, are the home of the just jurisprudents and the place on which professors and students from various countries descend. They are the souce of God's representatives (umana') and the successors of messengers. Whoever represents God among His servants and on His earth covets none of the ephemeral things of life obeys no order of the unjust, justifies no action of theirs, ties no knot for them and builds no edifice with them. You know what has been inflicted on Islam by the jurisprudents of the sultans and you know the impact that the jurisprudents who deal with the unjust have on the people. A jurisprudent working under the banner of the sultans causes more harm to Islam than any other ordinary individual working under their banner. This is why our infallible imams stressed this point and prohibited following the sultans and cooperating with the unjust rulers in any manner, regardless how insignificant, for fear that Islam and the Moslems would end up in the situation that we see at present.

The Imams, may peace be upon them, imposed on the jurisprudents very important ordinances and committed them to shouldering and preserving the trust. It is not right to resort to dissimulation on every issue, small and big. Dissimulation was legislated to preserve one's life or others from damage on subsidiary issues of the laws. But if Islam in its entirety is in danger, then there is no place for dissimulation and for silence. What do you think a jurisprudent should do if they force him to legislate or innovate? Do you think that he is permitted to cling to the imam's words "dissimulation is my religion and the religion of my fathers!" This is no place or situation for dissimulation. If dissimulation forces on of us to jump on the sultan's bandwagon then it should not be resorted to even if such refrainment leads to the death of the person concerned, unless his jumping on the bandwagon constitutes a real victory for Islam and the Moslems, as in the case of 'Ali ibn Yaqtin and Nasir-al-Din al-Tusi, may God have mercy upon their souls.

Naturally, our jurisprudents since the onset of Islam and until this day have been, as you know, above stooping to this level. The jurisprudents of the sultans were always from outside our group and always disagreed with us in opinion. Throughout the ages, our jurisprudents have been exposed to the ugliest forms of cruelty, persecution, annihilation and pursuit everywhere.

It is natural that Islam will permit joining the agencies of the unjust if the true purpose behind this is to curb injustice or to bring about a coup against those in charge. Such joining may even be a duty. We have no disagreement on this. Our criticism is addressed to those who have been motivated by greed, who have been lured by this earthly life, who have sold their hereafter for the world of others, who have been enticed by the devil to commit evil and who have worked for the treasonous rulers, supported and backed them and marched behind them, with God witnessing what they do and say.

Expel Jurisprudents of Sultans

These are no jurisprudents. Some of them have been given their turbans by the security and intelligence agencies so that they may beseech God and invoke His mercy and blessings for the sultan. Concerning such people, the Hadith says: "Beware of them for your religion."

These people must be exposed because they are the enemies of Islam. Society must renounce them because renouncing and despising them is a victory for Islam and for the cause of the Moslems. Our youths and sons must strip their turbans off their heads. Where are our youths in Iran? Have they died? I am not saying: Kill these people. But at least let their turbans be stripped away from them. All people must prevent such people from appearing in society in the garments of clergymen because this soils and desecrates this pure and noble garment. I have told you that the true Moslem ulema were held above such actions and they are still above such actions. Those whom you sometimes see and hear have glued themselves to the ulema by force when they have nothing to do with learning or with the ulema. They are a group of idle people. Others know them "and their account is written in a book with my God and God neither forgets nor errs."

We have been entrusted to polish ourselves and to steer them away from the ephemeral things of this world. As for you, prepare yourselves to preserve God's trust which He has placed in your hands. Be faithful to your religion and do not rely on this world or trust it. (You will not be able to have over your souls the control that your imam, the imam of the faithful to whom the world was not worth a goat's sneeze, had.) Turn away from what is guaranteed for you in this life, ennoble yourselves, fear your God and depend on Him. If you, God forbid, are studying the sciences of religion to rise in life, then I assure you that you will achieve nothing with God and will attain no commendable position. God will deny you the success in finding the virtue of interpretation, jurisprudence and insight into the laws of the religion and you will thus stop being the representatives of the messengers. Prepare yourselves to serve your religion and make yourselves ready for the imam of your time so that you may spread justice on the face of earth. Reform yourselves and take up the divine morals and the morals of the prophets. Leave the ornaments of life and be content with a life of sustenance so that people may follow the example of your abstinence and of the pride and loftiness of your souls and so that you may be a good model for them. Be God's soldiers and let the banners of Islam fly everywhere on your hands. I am not saying leave your studies, God forbid. Study and understand your religion deeply, warn your people and correct these theological academies and councils and do not allow them to collapse and fall. But while you are studying, inform, guide, direct and awaken the souls from their slumber. Islam at present is a stranger and there are no people who know it. Therefore, you must bring Islam closer to the people and you must explain it to them so that they may understand its true nature, without the doubts, suspicions and allegations created around it. Explain to the people the meaning of the Islamic government and the meaning of the message, the prophecy and the imamate. Why did Islam come? What does it want? Little by little, Islam will dwell in the hearts, the souls and the minds and then an Islamic government in which God's orders and strictures are embodied will rise.

Destroying Unjust Governments

1. Boycotting agencies of the unjust governments.

2. Abandoning cooperation with them.

3. Steering clear from any action that is of benefit to them.

4. Setting up new judiciary, financial, economic, cultural and political agencies.

We must fight the rule of the false god because God has ordered us to do so and has proscribed obedience to false gods or joining their bandwagons. The unjust authorities must vacate their place for the Islamic public services so that a stable and legitimate Islamic government may be established gradually.

God has urged us in His holy book to stand united like a firmly built edifice in the face of the unjust sultans. God ordered Moses to oppose and fight Pharoh. There are numerous Hadiths on this.

Our imams and their Shi'a have resisted tyrannical authorities throughout the ages in every place and they have never been on a truce with such authorities. Because of this, they have suffered extreme harm and persecution. This is evident to us from history which tells us about their lives.

Even though the imams were always under surveillance and were not permitted any freedom and even though they resorted to caution and dissimulation to preserve religion, and not themselves—despite all this, their words were not void of urging the people to resist and prohibiting them from observing a truce. The unjust rulers feared the guiding imams because they were aware that if the opportunity arose, the imams would rise to take control of affairs and would deny the rulers their life of luxury. You have seen Harun (al-Rashid) jail Imam Musa ibn Ja'far for long years and you have seen al-Ma'mun force Imam al-Rida to live in Maru under strict surveillance and then have him poisoned. This persecution was not because these men were the descendants of the prophet but because of the thoughts, opinions and positions that these people held. Harun and al-Ma'mun (pretended to support the Shi'a). However, their rule was futile and they were aware that 'Ali's descendants would claim the caliphate wherever they happened to be and would seek resolutely to form the Islamic government as part of their duties in life.

Al-Mahdi, an Abbaside caliph, asked Imam Musa ibn Ja'far about the borders of his property to return it to him and the imam outlined for him the borders of the entire Moslem countries saying: "One of the borders is Jahl Uhud, the other is al-'Arish of Egypt, the third is the coast of the sea and the fourth is Dawmat al-Jandal." Al-Mahdi said: "This is a lot. I will look into it."

The unjust ruler knew that if the imam wrenched his right from them, life would be denied them and that he would, if he found supporters, rise against them and never hesitate to do so. Have no doubt that Imam Musa ibn Ja'far would have taken the caliphate if the opportunity had presented itself and that he would have taken it to set matters aright, to defeat falsehood and to fill the world with justice.

Listen how al-Ma'mum appeased Imam al-Rida, gave him his assurance and addressed him as "cousin" and "son of God's messenger" and yet kept him under close surveillance because he feared from him for his power and because the imam had influence in the hearts of people, a place with God and relationship with the prophet. The sultans wanted rule and were ready to sacrifice everything for it. Had the imam gone along with them, God forbid, he would have lived a life of comfort and luxury and they would have kissed his hands and touched his feet for blessing all the time.

The Hadith says that when Imam al-Rida came to Harun, it was ordered that he enter the court riding his horse. When he came close to the caliph's podium, Harun rose to greet him and showed him utmost respect. But when Harun divided money among the people, he gave the Hashimites very little. This surprised al-Ma'mum (Harun's son) who was present at that council and who had seen the respect and veneration that his father had displayed toward the imam. So he asked his father about the reason for the little money he gave the Hashimites and the father said: "Son, you do not understand. The Hashimite share of this money should not exceed this. This matter belongs to them and they are more entitled to it than we are. If we let them, they will jump on us." Harun thus wanted the imams to remain poor, jailed, banished, homeless, killed and assassinated.

The imams were not alone in their fight against unjust authorities because they urged all the Moslems to do the same as they did. The books al-Wasa'il and Mustadrak al-Wasa'il contain more than fifty Hadiths ordering that tyrants and unjust rulers be shunned. In some of these Hadiths, the imams are ordered to throw dust in the faces and mouths of the panegyrists and say that whoever helps them, even if only with ink or a pen, shall suffer such and such evil and receive such and such punishment. In any case, we have been ordered to boycott and not to cooperate at all (with such rulers). On the other hand, there are Hadiths that urge learning and seeking knowledge and that praise learning, ulema and educated people. Some of these Hadiths say: "The ink of the learned people is better than the blood of the martyrs." All this is an open call for forming an Islamic government led by just jurisprudents to save the people from the yoke of colonialism and its lackeys and to erase all colonialist traces so that people may live under its canopy in safety and stability and so that they may know happiness in both worlds.

The Moslems will never at any time attain justice, security and stability until they acquire full faith and virtuous ethics under the canopy of a just government that follows the laws of Islam and dispenses with everything else.

We have been entrusted to present the thesis on Islamic government to the people and we hope that this thesis will evoke in the souls of people the awareness, zeal and vigilance on which the foundations and mainstays of the modern Islamic state are established so that the Moslems may regain their previous glory and dignity under its canopy. Glory to God, to his messenger and to the Moslems.

God keep from us the hands of the unjust, destroy the unjust rulers and kindle justice, mercy, compassion and vigilance in the souls of the Moslems so that they may work for the interest of their peoples and abandon their selfishness.

God give the youth, the educated and the university people success in implementing the sacred souls of Islam and unite all the Moslems so that they may rid themselves and resuce their nation from the talons of backwardness and the traces of colonialism. God give them success in defending their homeland in unity as if they are a firmly built edifice.

God give the jurisprudents and students of religious sciences knowledge, guidance and good works and make their efforts to set up the just Islamic state successful. You are the giver of success and there is no strength and no power without the great and almighty God.

GLOSSARY

'alim. A religious scholar.

amir. A prince, commander, or governor. Also a title given to the descendants of Mohammed (Muhammad).

ayatollah. Literally, the sign of God. The highest ecclesiastical order of Moslem in Iran.

caliph. A direct successor to the prophet.

hadith. The oral tradition of Islam; sayings or deeds attributed to Mohammad (Muhammad).

imam. A prayer leader and authority on Islamic law; a descendant of the House of Ali.

imamate. The mission of an imam.

infidel. A nonbeliever in Islam.

jihad. The holy war against the infidels; the struggle to establish the law of God.

jurisprudent. A jurist; a practitioner of the philosophy or science of the law.

Koran (Quran). The sacred text of Islam, believed to contain God's revelations to Mohammed (Muhammad).

muezzin. Crier who calls the faithful to prayer.

mullah. Title given to a Moslem leader.

sayyid. A descendant of Mohammed (Muhammad); title of respect for an Islamic dignitary.

ulema. The plural of 'alim.

waqf. Religious property; a permanent endowment or trust.

Shiite (Shi'a). The smaller of the two major divisions of Islam. Shiites support the House of Ali as the descendants to authority in Islam.

Sunni. The larger of the two major divisions of Islam. The Sunnis reject the House of Ali and follow the Koran (Quran) and the hadith.

George Carpozi Jr. is a prize-winning reporter and feature writer for the New York Post and one of the country's most prolific and widely-published authors.

In this, his 49th book, he provides us with a thorough analysis of the Iranian leader's concept of government and his intractably hostile stance against the United States.

Carpozi's previous venture into Arab world affairs was an absorbing biography of Egypt's President entitled:

MAN OF PEACE: ANWAR SADAT

Islamic Government
by Ayatollah Khomeini

An analysis by
George Carpozi Jr.

Like Adolph Hitler in another time, Ayatollah Ruhollah Khomeini is a tyrant, a hater, a baiter, a threat to world order and peace. The principal difference between the author of *Mein Kampf* and the compiler of the vapid *Islamic Government* is that one was an atheist while the other pretends to be a man of God.

It takes but one paragraph of his text on socio-economic, government, political, and technical developments in the countries of the Near East and North Africa to establish Khomeini's total preoccupation with the Hitlerian view of all followers of Judaism.

"Since its inception, the Islamic movement was afflicted with the Jews when they started their counter-activity by distorting the reputation of Islam, by assaulting it and by slandering it," writes the preposterous Ayatollah, who insists—even in the face of the historic cordiality that now exists between Israel and Egypt—that the condition "has continued to our present day."

He blames colonialist activity and domination for what he terms the "enemies' aim...to extinguish the flame of Islam and cause its vital revolutionary character to be lost so that the Moslems may not think of seeking to liberate themselves and to implement all the rules of their religion through the creation of a government that guarantees their happiness under the canopy of an honorable human life."

This is the thrust of his thesis from beginning to end, even as he plows through each of his many concepts about government, financial laws, the need for political revolution, the urgency for rescuing the wronged and deprived, and the qualifications of a ruler.

It is the irony of ironies that this man who spouts his absolute devotion to God, whom he calls "merciful" and "compassionate," is so diametrically different in his practices today as the dictatorial ruler of Iran.

He is a political leader with a fierce belief in his own mission, a religious fanatic who fantasizes that all foreigners are conspiring constantly to defame and denigrate his country and his religion.

"Islam possesses nothing," he groans about outsiders taunting his people. "Islam is nothing but a bunch of rules on menstruation and childbirth." But he admits that some theology students never go beyond those issues in their studies.

In the next breath, Khomeini exhibits still another aspect of the persecution complex he suffers. His paranoia is readily evident when he speaks of "the enemies, who have been working for hundreds of years to plant the seeds of negligence in our scientific academies so as to attain their goals in our wealth and in the resources of our country..."

Yet he makes no mention of, expresses no gratitude to the United States and the many other countries around the world which put the welcome mat out for thousands of Iranian students at colleges, universities, and other educational facilities.

He is an Iranian patriot who sees the world in stark moral terms. He is blinded in his anger and self-righteousness to such an extent that he harbors nothing but great pride in his own culture and corroding hatred for all foreign influences.

At the time that he wrote *Islamic Government* some ten years before the revolution which ousted the Shah Mohammed Riza Pahlevi and paved the way for the angry-faced 79-year-old Khomeini's return from his fifteen-year exile in Turkey, Iraq, and France, the Ayatollah appeared destined to remain away from his country for all time.

The hatred he holds for the Shah and his maniacal urge to murder the deposed ruler only points up Khomeini's total lack of charity and justice. The very man whose scalp he seeks spared the Ayatollah's life many times.

In 1944, Khomeini contributed to a book denouncing the monarchy, but the Shah overlooked this indiscretion, which, under Pahlevi's rulers, was a capital offense. Instead, the Ayatollah was put in charge of students at Qum and gained considerable favor among the young mullahs. Yet older pupils felt uneasy about the fervid professor and wanted little to do with him. He was too fanatic and too militant for them.

Khomeini had a brief moment in the sun in 1963 when members of the Moslem clergy tore Iran with demonstrations in protest of the Shah's "white revolution." That was the program of modernization which angered the mullahs because they, the second largest landholders in the country, did not profit from Pahlevi's land reform policies. Thier huge real estate holdings were distributed to the people.

Of the 1200 ayatollahs in the Shi'ite world, there are six who hold the title of Grand Ayatollah. The titles are not conferred by the religious hierarchy—as the election of Cardinals and Popes in the Vatican, for example—but by acclamation of the people, who are inclined to turn to the religious leader they admire most.

Among the Grand Ayatollahs at the time of the 1963 religious riots, only Khomeini steadfastly demanded the Shah's overthrow and adamantly refused to compromise even after more than two hundred Moslems were killed in the streets.

The Shah, whose might then was unassailable, despite the turmoil the religious community had visited on the country, could have very easily brought Khomeini before a firing squad and ended all the future grief Pahlevi was fated to endure.

Instead, the Shah exiled Khomeini, who found asylum first in Turkey, then Iraq; the Iraqi government finally expelled him in October, 1978, a few short months before the Shah was deposed and Khomeini returned triumphant and virtually in full control of the country, although he insisted it was not his intention to rule Iran and that he would turn over the reins of government to a political leader whom he would select.

Khomeini tells us a ruler must have a thorough knowledge of the Islamic law and of justice, besides possessing "general qualifications, such as intelligence, maturity, and a good sense of management."

He speaks of a need to dispense justice "with a sound faith and good ethics." Yet in the first year of his return he dispensed justice for thousands before the firing squad, instigated the seizure of the American embassy and its sixty-two hostages in one of the most barbaric acts in modern history, and demanded the return of the Shah so he could be put to death.

There's little doubt about whom the Ayatollah speaks of when he states:

"God brings to account unjust rulers and every government deviating from the teachings of Islam. He makes them account for what they gained, for how they spent the monies of the Moslems, for the monies they wasted on coronation ceremonies, and on the 25th centennial anniversary of the rule of sultans in Iran."

Then Khomeini asks, "What will they say when they are brought to account?"

As though peering into the future, into a time capsule that will one day open and sprout a Mohammed Riza Pahlevi sitting in the witness chair on judgement day, Khomeini takes it upon himself to testify for the Shah:

"Perhaps he will apologize and say: 'Our special circumstances made this inevitable and called for building the biggest palaces and for excessive and unchecked extravagance in coronation anniversaries and similar occasions for the sake of fame and reputation in the world.' "

It is interesting to follow the questioning further, for if a time should come and the deposed Shah returns to Teheran to face the music, we may have here a verbatim transcript of precisely the questions the trial judges will ask:

Was not 'Ali a good example for you?

Have you done for the people more than the amir of the faithful did for them?

Did you want to elevate Islam to a status to which 'Ali had not elevated it?

In effect, this vengeful fanatic, obsessed with the idea of rebuilding his country into the fanatic Islamic community it was at its birth twenty-five centuries ago, and is willing to wipe out all the progress of the last forty years and revert to the listless society the Iranian people had before the Shah's modernization program introduced the advantages of Western civilization.

From exile, Khomeini's rage reached volcanic fury as he watched Pahlevi's transformation of the conservative Islamic tradition that the Ayatollah espouses into an up-to-date society—although it had not yet done away with its traditional authoritarianism and corruption.

From the earliest of times, when he challenged monarchic rule as being in conflict with Islamic rule and with the Islamic political system, Khomeini was especially infuriated by the "foreign laws" which "caused the Moslem society numerous problems."

He doesn't sound irrational, however, in this justifiable challenge to the Iranian justice system:

"...whoever is involved in a judiciary or legal case in Iran, or in similar states, must spend a long life to win such a case." He quotes a lawyer saying to him: "I can keep a case between two disputants in the courts all my life and it is most likely that my son will succeed me to the case."

The Ayatollah also takes the justice system apart for "the illicit profits that people with influence gain from their cases through trickery, perfidy, bribery, deception, and cheating."

He cites the hardships defendants and litigants must endure and suggests that cases once tried under the old Islamic laws and dispensed with in a couple or three days now take twenty years to settle. He complains with a reasonable voice:

"During this time, a young man turns old for having to check with the judiciary authorities morning and evening, having to roam their halls hopelessly and for having to be brought back to these authorities and halls whenever he wants to leave them."

His voice also rings with logic when he takes exception to the inordinate criticism by Americans and other Western societies of Islamic justice which punishes an alcohol drinker with eighty whip lashes, an unmarried adulterer with one hundred lashes, and a married adulterer or adulteress with stoning.

"I wonder how these people think," Khomeini says. "They carry out the death sentence, under the pretext of the law, against several people for smuggling ten grams of heroin....When they legislate these inhumane laws under the pretext of preventing corruption, they see no harshness in them."

Of course the Ayatollah says he doesn't condone dealing in heroin but opposes the death penalty for those who traffic in the drug.

"Dealing in heroin," he suggests, "must be fought, but on a basis compatible with the dimensions of the crime."

Still on the course of criticism against those who would condemn Islamic law for its cruelty and harshness of punishment meted to alcohol drinkers and adulterers, Khomeini demands to know why no one objected to the "bloody massacres that have been taking place in Vietnam...?"

Evidently he hadn't heard of Jane Fonda at the time he was writing his *Islamic Government*.

Khomeini is acutely aware of the audience he is reaching—the youth of Islam whom he has always favored with his teachings—and he imparts many wise pearls of wisdom. He is an astute historian and as such harps on the past injustices visited upon Iran's masses.

"You, the youths who are the soldiers of Islam," he preaches, "must examine more thoroughly the brief statements I am making to you and must familiarize people throughout your life with the laws and rules of Islam and must do so with every possible means: In writing, in speeches, and in actions.

"Teach the people about the catastrophes, tragedies, and enemies that have engulfed Islam since its inception. Do not hide what you know from the people and do not let people imagine that Islam is like present-day Christianity, that there is no difference between the mosque and the church and that Islam can do no more than regulate man's relationship with his God."

His outspokenness about the *differences* which he maintains exist between Mohammedanism and Christianity is a signal that he considers his religion more absolute and far-reaching. He refers to a time when "darkness prevailed over the Western countries, when American Indians were inhabiting America," and he touches on the Roman and Persian empires which, he charges, practiced domination and racial discrimination, as well as "excessive use of force with total disregard" for either public opinion or the laws that existed.

Khomeini tells us, in that very period of world history, God spoke to Mohammed and laid down the laws by which man must live. This view forecloses the possibility of giving equal or even partial credit to Christianity for having such broad goals, because Jesus' teachings in the Bible are not the laws universally adopted by governments in the world. Constitutions, Magna Carters, and other organs pronouncing the shape and thrust of nations do not enslave themselves to the Bible as Islam does to the Moslem sacred scripture, the Koran, which professes to record the revelations of Allah (God) to Mohammed.

The Ayatollah stresses this fact when he asserts:

"Rights in Islam are high-level, complete and comprehensive rights. Jurists have often quoted the Islamic rules, laws, and regulations on dealings, on permissibles, punishment, jurisdiction, on regulating relations between states and peoples, on war and peace, and on human rights."

Thus, he claims, Mohammedanism is a broad canopy unravelled by Allah and designed to deal with every aspect of life from every Islamic's birth and "until the time he is lowered into his grave." Khomeini is unequivocal in his discourse on this subject and he goes into a frenzy lashing at the "colonialists" who, he rails, infiltrated Islam centuries ago with the avowed purpose of corrupting the populace and destroying its religion and culture.

"At the outset, they established a school somewhere. We did not lift a finger and we, and people like us, failed to prevent this. These schools increased gradually and now you find that they have advocates in all the villages."

The ultimate indignity, the Ayatollah says, is that this foreign influence has had the effect of leading children away from their religion, as well as keeping Iranians "backward, weak, and miserable."

But Khomeini makes no mention of the countless shiploads of medical supplies, the limitless flow of food, and the many other beneficial supplies that the "foreigners" brought to his country by which they improved the state of health as well as the life spans of his people.

The Ayatollah doesn't view industrial and scientific advances as yardsticks of progress or of achievement. He suffers a distinct aberration in this regard and rejects Western attainments as irrelevant challenges which visit a sense of inferiority upon Iranians.

Such accomplishments tend to make his countrymen "grow smaller and to think that our failure to do the same is due to our religion and its laws and to violate the Islamic teachings and beliefs."

He speaks about America's moon landings and assumes the posture that the "enemies" did not reach this "magnificent advance in invading outer space" because of the West's laws.

"Let them go to Mars or anywhere they wish," he carps. "They are still backward in the sphere of securing happiness to man, backward in spreading moral virtues and backward in creating a psychological and spiritual progress similar to the material progress.

"They are still unable to solve their social problems because solving these problems and eliminating hardship requires an ideological and moral spirit."

To that end, the Ayatollah enunciates with considerable stress that "wealth, capabilities, and resources," such as those that brought about the material gains of conquering space, require the Islamic faith, creed, and ethics to provide the ultimate in balance and fulfillment. Only the Islamic faith, he insists, provides the proper equanimity of morals and laws, and if the populace unshackles itself from Western influences and mores it will wipe out injustice and poverty.

This Moslem cleric who believes so deeply in his religion can be understood, it seems, only in the context of his religious tradition, the Shi'ite branch of Islam. This branch is strongly influenced by Oriental mysticism and authoritarianism, and places extreme emphasis on martyrdom.

Before the fighting that toppled the Shah and opened the way for Ayatollah Khomeini's return and his effective seizure of the government, he had sent word from exile to his followers:

"Put on white robes so the blood from your wounds will show better..."

While in Paris just before the monarchy was overthrown in Iran, Khomeini referred to his advanced age and the brief time remaining to him. It has been suggested the Ayatollah may be seeking, on a psychological level, some sort of martyrdom, final proof of the spiritual or religious quality of the revolution he spawned.

In a "personality assessment" psychological profile of Khomeini prepared by the Central Intelligence Agency's National Foreign Assessments Center, the religious despot is viewed in this vein:

"Khomeini is an old man preoccupied with the fact that he will live at best only a few more years. He believes he must do what would take a century in two or three years.

"He must make the changes he ordains a permanent part of Iranian society while he lives, because he cannot trust those who come after him to keep the faith.

"This gives a frenzied intensity to all of Khomeini's actions."

The study pointed out that the Ayatollah sees himself as a restorer of militant Islam to its state at the time of origin twenty-five centuries past.

His unwillingness to compromise is rooted in a sense of personal Messianic mission, and his anti-American fervor is without doubt the outgrowth of those fifteen lost years in banishment from his native land.

He holds the United States personally responsible for keeping Pahlevi in power and isolating the Ayatollah from the Iranian people. But his hatred for the royal family actually goes back to his early childhood. Let's trace that background so that we may be better informed about certain influences which led the bearded cleric into his corrosive hatred of the Shah, as well as of all Western civilizations—but most of all the United States.

Ruhollah Khomeini was born Ruhollah Hendi on

May 17, 1900, in the village of Khomein, near Isfahan in central Iran. He was the youngest of six children born to his father, Mustafa, an Ayatollah, and his mother, who also came from a clerical family.

Khomeini's father died when Ruhollah was only six months old, leaving him to the care of his strong-willed, devout mother, and a big, protective brother, Alameh Seyed Morteza Moosavi.

His father's death had a profound effect on Ruhollah because Mustafa was killed by the mayor of the village in a personal clash precipitated by an argument over the viability of Reza Shah, the father of the now-exiled Shah Pahlevi.

From the time he was old enough to sense his personal loss in that tragedy, Ruhollah Hendi acquired a bitter malevolence toward the monarchy. Ruhollah was thirty years old in 1930 when he decided to disown his family name. One of his brothers was arrested for leftist activities and Ruhollah, playing it safe, took a new last name—Khomeini, an adaptation from the name of the village of Khumain, his birthplace.

Ayatollah Khomeini has had two wives. His first one, now dead, bore him a son, Mustafa, born in 1933. With his second wife, daughter of a rich landowner from Gilan Province, he had a second son, Ahmad, and three daughters.

If Khomeini's bitterness and hatred against the Shah's rule was ever brought to volcanic boil it was in 1978 when Mustafa, who also studied theology and attained the rank of Ayatollah, died in mysterious circumstances in Iraq. Reports hinted that the Shah's secret police killed Khomeini's son despite an official version that he died of natural causes at the age of forty.

The CIA psychological profile takes note of that tragic event and attributes more to it than anything else for bringing about the most dramatic change in the Ayatollah's personality.

"Khomeini was a lonely old man in exile," the CIA report states. "The exile was a painful, heart-rending separation for a man who drew his identity from contact with Iranian life.

"The Iran that Khomeini came back to was nothing like the Iran he left. He has difficulty understanding how the country could have changed so much.

"After Khomeini's son died, the gentleness went out of him. He is motivated by revenge..."

Perhaps no better example can be found of his intentions to visit grief and injury upon the United States, which he blames most for the changes in Iran, than the views he expressed when Pope John Paul II sent an envoy to Ayatollah Khomeini to discuss the situation at the American Embassy in Tehran, where Islamic students held the sixty-two American hostages prisoners in the U.S. Embassy.

Khomeini agreed to meet the Pontiff's emissary because, as the Ayatollah put it, "due to our respect for Christian clerics and the Pope..." But he was merely talking out of the side of his mouth, as it turned out.

The Ayatollah cited "the weight of American imperialism" that assertedly had brought "suffering" to Iran's 35 million people. He also mentioned the "special pressure" exerted by President Jimmy Carter to free the hostages—the White House had sent delegates to European allies to turn the screws on Iran.

But then Khomeini turned on the Pope himself and

took him to task. Listen to this diatribe as he refers to the "millions of impoverished masses throughout the world" who, he said, "long expected some form of consolation from the Pope," and takes this slap at John Paul:

"They expected a paternal gesture of soothing from the Pope and were hopeful that the Pope should have warned the oppressors against all acts of injustice and counted on him as a figure who would mediate between the impoverished nations and the superpowers who claim to be Christians.

"But alas the cries of the impoverished masses always fell on deaf ears. We gave our lives over a period of fifty years. Our people were massacred in masses. They imprisoned our people and tortured them in jails in a most inhumane manner. In those days, no person would even venture to mediate. Never did it occur to the great Pope to defend the rights of these impoverished peoples. Never did it occur to him to act as a mediator so that this nation of impoverished masses could be left alone."

The Ayatollah justified the Embassy takeover by the students because, he charged, the diplomatic outpost of the U.S. was a "den of spies" which carried out widespread acts of espionage against the Iranian people and the Middle East. He questioned the quick shredding and burning of documents and files as the invaders broke down the gates and suggested that these papers were the products of Embassy subversive activity against Iran.

"If all these documents were related to normal Embassy activity and if they did not reveal what they did, that is, conspiracy against our nation, our people would not have resorted to such action. But now that we have been convinced of a plot which was in the making against our country, and now that our people here along with people in other countries have supported the occupation of the Embassy by our youth, I must remind you that this move has been the will of the entire Iranian nation and that this action must not be construed as having been taken solely by the insistence of a group of youths."

The Ayatollah mentioned no nation by name that was in sympathy with the Embassy takeover—and, in fact, none was. But Khomeini makes his own rules and establishes his own parameters and paradigms.

The Ayatollah's criticism of the Pope was an example of the type of insensitivity and inaccuracy many of Khomeini's phrases carry. John Paul had only been at the seat of Roman Catholic power in the Vatican for barely longer than a year when Khomeini took his swipes at the Pontiff. The angry old man ranted on and on...

"I am now surprised to see that only at a time like this the great Pope has been moved to such an extent that he wants to see them (the hostages) freed in the name of humanity. Well, as far as the conduct of our people with the hostages is concerned, I can only say our youth are Moslems and that to my knowledge their conduct with them has been in keeping with human principles and there remains nothing for you to worry about.

"As for the releasing of these people, one must first clearly see what we want and what our people want of us."

Of course, the major demand was the return of the

Shah, who at that very moment was convalescing from surgery in a New York City hospital after removal of gall stones and radiation therapy for a malignant cancer growth on his neck.

The Ayatollah poses a rhetorical question as to whether holding the hostages was an illegal act —when the motivation was driven by "unselfish and humane feelings?"

Without mentioning the Shah's name, Khomeini lashes into the desposed monarch with his most potent verbal artillery:

"It is, therefore, worth recalling that our people have been subjected to such torment by that person who is now in the United States. He committed all forms of treason for a period of thirty-seven years. During this period our youth were deprived of a decent living. For a period of thirty-seven years this nation was subjected to oppression from all quarters under the plans devised and engineered by this very person.

"For example, he massacred innumerable people on June 5, 1963. Since then he has probably killed more than 100,000 people. As a result of his brutality, thousands of others have also been injured.

"In the face of this suffering our nation now demands the extradiction of this criminal to Iran to be tried on the basis of the principles of justice.

"If he is convicted he should give back the property that he has taken from us. Right now the wealth that he and his relatives have taken from this country is overflowing in banks in the United States and Western countries."

There's very little question about the Shah's wealth. He is reputed to have skimmed anywhere from $2 billion to $10 billion and even more for himself and his family. On that count alone, we should all agree he is a first class crook. So no matter how much progress and advancement he has brought to Iran, that cannot exonerate him for being a glutton, a thief, and a killer.

Ayatollah Khomeini wasn't about to let up on the Shah with that last statement. The grizzled cleric was merely winding up. His next delivery went like this:

"I know for a fact, and people my age have, and those who have studied history will confirm this, that when his father launched a coup d'etat, he had nothing. He was a mere soldier. But when he started to dominate the country he began to confiscate people's property.

"The best farms in Mazandaran, north in Iran, came into his possession by the force of his agents. Many of the owners or religious leaders who expressed an opinion on this matter were imprisoned or sometimes killed.

"I remember during the reign of Reza Shah that people were massacred in the Goharshad Mosque (in Mashhad) where they had gathered for prayers to God, and that a number of oppressed people who had gathered in the mosque were also killed.

"When he left Iran, or rather was thrown out, he took with him his country's jewels, as much as he could put in his suitcases. However, during his sea journey, the British took away all the jewels from him.

"When it was time to do so, the Allied Powers imposed his criminal son (Mohammed Reza Pahlevi) upon our nation, given the fact that the Iranian nation was not receptive to the son after what they had seen from the father."

The Ayatollah heaped nothing but condemnation upon the son...

"...this man provided everything they (the allies) demanded. The treacheries he has committed during his reign with respect to our people are too numerous to be counted. As an example, one of the services he performed was to purchase arms and ammunition in exchange for the oil the country exported to the United States. These weapons were subsequently geared for the American military bases. Thus, this man gave away our oil and with its money he built bases for others.

"Also during the past ten or fifteen years he killed many of our youth. His prisons were full of young patriots..."

Departing from a proper discourse on the Shah's liabilities, now once more Ayatollah Khomeini took another cheap shot at Pope John Paul II:

"During this period we would have liked to have heard a word from one of the spiritual leaders abroad, especially the great Christian leader, in sympathy with this oppressed nation. I cannot believe that the Vatican was unaware of what was happening here. I do not know what to do about this anomaly when people wonder if the Christian clergy agreed with these crimes. I do not know what to tell them.

"The Christian clergy know very well that the Holy Quran has defended the Virgin Mary and has strongly rejected the calumnies that had been hurled against her.

"Thus the Quran has defended Christianity and its religious leaders and Saints. We would have liked to see personalities like the Pope inquire for once why our nation was undergoing such suffering, and to ask

Carter why he is now playing host to a man whose crime and treacheries of more than thirty years are quite evident, so that he may once again indulge in plots and intrigues."

The Ayatollah was vitriolic as he next zeroed in on President Carter:

"We are not surprised by Carter's moves. He is a politician, not in the healthy sense of politics, but in his own way. He commits any treachery to fulfill his personal interests, under the illusion that he is serving his country's interest, and so that our youth may not see the facts.

"But I wonder why the Pope offers to intervene in this affair in which an oppressed nation wants to become further aware of some of the injustices done to it, and to be able to tell other oppressed peoples of the kind of oppressions it has been subjected to. It merely wants to put the oppressor on trial.

"We would have taken the initiative if we could try this man (the deposed Shah) in another country. But the crimes he has committed, the documents we have on him, and the millions of witnesses we have—the farmers, workers, clergy, and academicians who have been oppressed—we cannot take over twenty million people abroad as witnesses. But as a sign of the respect we have for the Pope, we would welcome his representative and that of any other individual, even a representative of our worst enemy, Carter, to attend this man's trial in this country. Whatever the Court's verdict, our people will abide by it..."

The Ayatollah offered yet another message to the Pontiff.

"I would like the Pope to know that this is not an

issue that I may be able to solve personally," Khomeini rattled. "We do not want to impose anything on the nation. Islam does not permit anyone to be a dictator. We submit to the people's will. The Almighty God and the Prophet of Islam do not authorize us to impose anything on our people. We may occasionally put a humble request to the people. It is in the hands of the nation. And the nation has expressed in support for this action. As you may be aware, Radio Iran has been announcing the endless support of various segments of the population."

The Ayatollah took this break in his liturgy to interpose:

"In any case our issue is a humanitarian one. Because of their adherence to Islam our people are humanitarian. And you as a Christian should follow the example of Christ and be humanitarian just as Jesus was..."

The bottom line, Khomeini tells us, is that his people don't want Pahlevi put on trial for revenge, but rather so the world "may know who motivated him in committing these crimes of oppression, and plundering our resources, and thus, other nations may learn from this example."

Again, speaking of the evils the Shah committed during his reign—the massacres, the deployment of wealth, and the deprivations of shelter, bread, and work—Khomeini presumes to suggest that even John Paul would not ask for the hostages' freedom once he is apprised of the cruelty of the Shah's rule.

"If he has not yet heard about this," the Ayatollah ranted, "we now inform him about what he (the ex-Shah) has done. In the face of all these facts I do not suspect that the Pope will suggest that we set free these people without having this individual (the ex-Shah) at our disposal, and I do not think that the Pope will issue such a judgment.

"Why?

"Because the Pope, like any other human being is certainly aware of these crimes. At any rate we do not have an illegitimate demand. Every human being, in any part of the world, with the exception of the person of Carter, who lends his ears to our demand, will accept it."

Khomeini labels his demand a fair one.

"We say you have taken our criminal and you are giving him refuge. We want you to surrender him to us. He is the same person who killed our youth, who roasted our young people in boiling pots, who charred them on fire, and who cut their limbs.

"We demand that you surrender this person to us so that we may give him a fair trial..."

Now the Ayatollah really comes along with a gasser:

"Should it be proven that our claims are unfounded, then we will put him back on the Peacock Throne, in which case the people of this country will obey him."

From this ludicrous assertion Khomeini flips to another one as he implores the Pope to become Iran's emissary in the campaign to return the Shah:

"It is only fitting at a time like this that he (the Pope) show some concern about the dignity of the Christian world. It remains his duty to reveal the true identity of the people who preach the gospel but who act against it.

"The Pope must now reveal Mr. Carter to the people of the United States and to the world of Christianity, and he must enumerate the latter's crimes for them, as we have done with Mohammed Reza. Naturally, our people had long since known the truth about him, but despite this, we do our best to disclose more about him, and we expect you to do the same.

"If you do this we will appreciate it. We are bringing our plea to you because we have been subject to injustice. We call on the Christian world to redeem itself. Because of what these people in the larger countries do in the name of the Messiah, and the crimes they commit in the name of Christianity they are thus not consistent with the spirit of Christ.

"Such acts serve only to disgrace Christians the world over. Let me reassure the Pope that had Jesus Christ been living today, he would have reprimanded Mr. Carter.

"Were Jesus living today he would have rescued us from the claws of this enemy of the people. You are his representative and in your capacity we expect you to do what Jesus Christ would have done had he been living today..."

There is one fatal flaw in Ayatollah Khomeini's references to Jesus Christ. He has either deliberately chosen to ignore or is so misinformed about Christianity that he does not know about this Messiah. The Iranian leader repeatedly forecloses against the belief of every Christian—that Jesus does indeed live. So when this follower of Mohammed says "were Jesus living today," he is in effect delivering a purposefully blasphemous slap at all Christianity.

The Ayatollah does not seem to be aware—or doesn't want to show his knowledge—about the universally-accepted Christian concept that the Cross was not the end of Jesus. That God rescued Him from death—and that is why the Christian world uniformly observes the Resurrection with the celebration of Easter.

But this should not surprise anyone after what we've analyzed here thus far about Ayatollah Khomeini's views on *Islamic Government*—truly an Arabian *Mein Kampf*—and his more recent stance on the seizing of the hostages and his adamant refusal to free them.

He is one of the most contrary national leaders the world has ever known. Perhaps his view of the Islamic system of government in his book a decade ago no longer holds in present times to his postulation of that bygone era:

"The Islamic government is not similar to the well-known system of government. It is not a despotic government in which the head of state dictates his opinion and tampers with the lives and property of the people. The prophet...and 'Ali, the amir of the faithful, and the other imams had no power to tamper with people's property or with their lives.

"The Islamic government is not despotic but constitutional..."

Oh, yeah? What about the thousands executed by firing squad since Khomeini deposed the Shah?

The Ayatollah concedes, however, that the Islamic government isn't constitutional "in the well-known sense of the word."

He tells us Islamic government doesn't function in the same way as in the parliamentary system or in the people's councils. Rather, he ascribes to it his definition of constitutional government "in the sense that those in charge of affairs observe a number of conditions and rules underlined in the Koran and in the Sunna and represented in the necessity of observing the system and of applying the dictates and laws of Islam."

And that is why Islamic government, the Ayatollah insists, is "government of the divine law." He then spells out the ultimate difference between Islamic and constitutional governments, whether monarchic or republican:

"The people's representatives or the king's representatives are the ones who codify and legislate, whereas (under Islamic rule) the power of legislation is confined to God...and nobody else has the right to legislate and nobody may rule by that which has not been given power by God.

"This is why Islam replaces the legislative council (the legislative, judiciary, and executive powers) by a planning council that works to run the affairs and work of the ministries so that they may offer their services in all spheres."

If there's doubt in any mind that the Ayatollah wants to wipe away twenty-five centuries of Iranian history and bring the country back to its origins, then this passage from his analysis of *Islamic Government* should erase everyone's lingering irresolution:

"All that is mentioned in the book (Koran) and in the Sunna is acceptable and obeyed in the view of the Moslems. This obedience facilitates the state's responsibilities, whereas when the majorities in the constitutional monarchic or republican governments legislate something, the government has to later exert efforts to compel people to obey, even if such obedience requires the use of force.

"The Islamic government is the government of the law and God alone is the ruler and the legislator. God's rule is effective among all the people and in the state itself.

"All individuals—the prophet, his successors, and other people—follow what Islam, which descended through revelation and which God has explained through the Koran and through the words of His prophet, has legislated for them."

That means there must be no further legislation to meet changing population needs, modern advances, and changing world conditions. At least there should not be, in the Ayatollah Khomeini's scheme of things.

"The venerable prophet," Khomeini claims, was appointed ruler on earth by God "so that he may rule justly and not follow whims."

God, the Ayatollah says further, addressed the prophet "through revelation and told him to convey what was revealed in him to those who would succeed him."

The prophet obeyed that commandment and appointed 'Ali as his successor.

"He was not motivated in this appointment by the fact that 'Ali was his son-in-law and the fact that 'Ali had performed weighty and unforgettable services, but because God ordered the prophet to do so."

Thus, according to the Ayatollah, government in Islam "means obeying the law and making it the judge."

He quotes God after he assertedly ordered the prophet and the rulers after him: "Obey the prophet and those in charge among you." Then Khomeini launches into a deep and philosophical overview of Islamic government in which he reviews his country's past, from the beginning. He decries the big palaces, servants, royal courts, crown prince courts, and "other trivial requirements that consume half or most of the country's resources and that the sultans and the emperors have."

Khomeini speaks of the "life of utter simplicity" that the great prophet pursued even though he enjoyed the power of supreme ruler.

"This method continued to a degree after him and until the Ommiads seized power. The government of 'Ali ibn Abi Talib was a government of reform...'Ali lived a life of utter simplicity while managing a vast state in which Iran, Egypt, Hejaz, and Yemen were mere provinces under his rule.

"I do not believe that any of our poor people can live the kind of life that the imam ('Ali) lived. When he had two cloaks, he gave the better one to Qanbar, his servant, and he wore the other. When he found extra material in his sleeves, he cut it off.

"Had this course continued until the present, people would have known the state of happiness and the country's treasury would not have been plundered to be spent on fornication, abomination, and the court's costs and expenditures.

"You know that most of the corrupt aspects of our society are due to the corruption of the ruling dynasty and the royal family."

Ayatollah Ruhollah Khomeini overlooked that this very policy of sharing his worldly goods that 'Ali demonstrated was also the practice of Shah Mohammed Riza Pahlevi. The Shah shared all his worldly goods with his wife, his sister, his children, and other members of his family. Generously.

The Ayatollah's seventy-four single-spaced type-written manuscript of *Islamic Government,* as translated into English by the Joint Publications Research Service, is a thoroughly enlightening report on Khomeini's interpretation of the Islamic movement in Iran. Yet it is overly cumbersome and annoyingly repetitious.

It is the work product of an angry man, one whose years of waiting to return to his native land and assume the role of highest religious authority have made him unreasonably vile, vituperative, and vapid.

It is not a scholarly work. Rather, it has all the elements one might expect from an obsessed pamphleteer. He rages too much, rants too often, cries for revenge against the Shah with monotonous frequency. Yet, strangely, he never once mentions by name the man he despises with a corrosive passion.

Not until he returns to power do his lips shape the Shah Pahlevi's identity. Then the angry Ayatollah breaks into full gallop against the Shah when he responds to Pope John Paul's plea to release the hostages.

Next to the Shah, President Carter seems to be Khomeini's most hated foe. That comes across with crystal clearness when the Ayatollah discusses the President's efforts to emancipate the hostages. After voicing assurances that the captive Embassy staff is not in danger and is being kept in comfort, Khomeini lashes at the Chief Executive:

"Mr. Carter has resorted to everything possible to rescue himself from this entanglement. He has been acting like a drowning person who will cling to anything that comes his way.

"Once he endeavors to threaten us with an impending military move. Another time, he says that he will impose economic sanctions against us..."

Khomeini is a wiley fox when it comes to lining up enemies for his followers to hate passionately. Now he drags one of the Shah's top advisers and aides, Shahpur Bakhtiar. Follow the Ayatollah's method of connecting the former minister with the Shah and the President:

"It is unfortunate that in the midst of these developments (the economic sanctions) a person who claims to be Iranian and who says he is first an Iranian and then a Moslem, should ask Carter to exercise economic boycotts against Iran."

The Ayatollah mentions Bakhtiar by name, then rants:

"He is now in England and claims to be a nationalistic figure. Now you see how my past prediction has come true today. Sometime ago I said something which is being realized today. I recall I said that the superpowers might support a person for twenty or thirty years so that they may use him on a rainy day, so that they can make a servant out of him, and make him their agent, by presenting him in the disguise of a national figure, like Bakhtiar, who has apparently attached himself to the late Dr. Mossadegh and who claims to be nationalistic.

"They use such people when the time is ripe for them. He was a member of the National Front for many years and claimed to be concerned about the nation. He said he was first an Iranian and second a 'Moslem,' a statement which is in itself blasphemy.

"But at the time when they needed him, they used

him and he continued the mass killings once he had replaced the most wicked creature of God, who was Mohammed Reza, he ordered his men to kill our people, except that his men did not obey his orders.

"He (Bakhtiar), too, has proposed that a state of economic seige should be imposed on this country."

All that verbal onslaught is relatively harmless and it could be chalked up to the bombasts of a splenetic old man who has but a few weeks, months, or at most a handful of years left to disrupt the world order.

But then he enters another realm—he suggests what he and his countrymen are ready to handle military intervention, if it should come to that over the hostages.

"Let me announce here that we are neither afraid of military interference nor are we afraid of economic seige, since we are Shi'ites and as Shi'ites we welcome any opportunity for sacrificing our blood. Our nation looks forward to an opportunity for self-sacrifice and martyrdom.

"Now let us suppose that in the absence of all reasoning, Mr. Carter or perhaps the superpowers should agree to send military forces here. Well, then, we have a population of 35 million, most of whom long for martyrdom.

"We will go to battle with all these 35 million people, and once we are all martyred, then our enemies can do whatever they want to do with this country.

"We are not afraid of such an encounter. We are men of war, we are born to struggle. Our youth have fought against army tanks and machine guns with bare hands. Mr. Carter need not frighten us of any warlike encounter. We are men of war even though we may go